MW01078578

THE BEST OF STORE DESIGNS

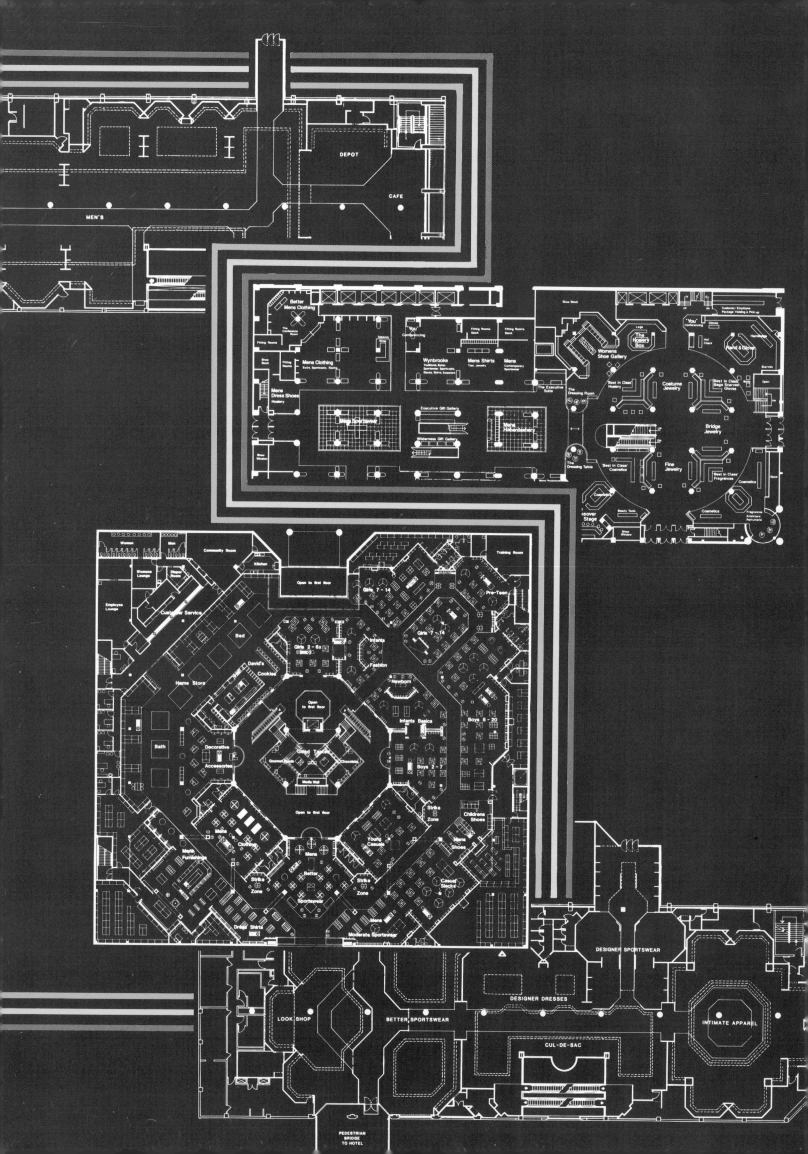

THE BEST OF STORE DESIGNS

From **National Retail Merchants Association**
and the **Institute for Store Planners'**
Store Interior Design Competition

PBC International Inc. ● New York

Copyright © 1986 by PBC International, Inc.
All rights reserved. No part of this book may be reproduced in any
form whatsoever without written permission of the copyright owner,
PBC International, Inc., P.O. Box 678, Locust Valley, NY 11560.

Distributors to the trade in the United States:
PBC International, Inc.
P.O. Box 678
Locust Valley, NY 11560

Distributors to the trade in Canada:
General Publishing Co. Ltd.
30 Lesmill Road
Don Mills, Ontario, Canada M3B 2T6

Distributed in Continental Europe by:
Fleetbooks, S.A.
Feffer and Simons, B.V.
170 Rijnkade
Weesp, Netherlands

Distributed throughout the rest of the world by:
Fleetbooks, S.A.
c/o Feffer and Simons, Inc.
100 Park Avenue
New York, NY 10017

Library of Congress Cataloging in Publication Data
Main entry under title:

Store designs.

    Includes index.
    1. Store decoration—United States.   2. Department stores—United
States—Designs and plans.   I. National Retail Merchants
Association.   II. Institute of Store Planners (U.S.)
Planners (U.S.)
NK2195.S89S7.4   1985   725'.21'0973   85-6445
ISBN 0-86636-012-3

Color separation, printing, and binding by
Toppan Printing Co. (H.K.) Ltd. Hong Kong

Typesetting by David E. Seham Associates Inc.
Metuchen, New Jersey

PRINTED IN HONG KONG

10 9 8 7 6 5 4 3 2 1

Publisher: Hero Taylor
Project Director: Cora S. Taylor
Managing Editor: Steve Blount
Editor: Carol Denby
Art Director: Richard Liu
Art Associates: Charlene Sison
Daniel Kouw
Daniel Larkin

CONTENTS

FOREWORD

For a number of years, NRMA has planned on publishing a book on excellence in store interior design. The reason is simple: In an age of constant change, the retail enterprise, if it is to survive, must possess an individuality all its own. Some call it theatre.

Theatre comes in many different shapes and sizes. The intermarriage of ideas with talent has given us a new generation of store designer and a new generation of store design. Hence, the smallest specialty shop today can, and often does, possess an atmosphere and environment as uniquely distinguishable as that of a major department store.

The challenge of store interior design is constant visual stimulation. To be selected for an award in the ISP/NRMA Store Interior Design Competition, a designer or

firm must create an outstanding
environment which enhances and attracts
the shopping public. The designer's product
must never reflect boredom or repetition.
The winning designs on these pages
exceeded these standards and challenges.

Enjoy your copy of **THE BEST OF STORE
DESIGNS.** We hope it will be a source of
inspiration in your own pursuit of the
"best" in store design.

James R. Williams, President,
NATIONAL RETAIL MERCHANTS ASSOCIATION

INTRODUCTION

Store interior designers have often remained unrecognized. We realize their importance but quite often fail to acknowledge their overall contributions to the success of the retail enterprise.

This book, **"THE BEST OF STORE DESIGNS",** a combined effort of the National Retail Merchants Association and the Institute of Store Planners, focuses attention on those outstanding people and firms whose work has been selected by qualified judges to receive the annual 1984 ISP/NRMA Interior Design Awards.

Equally important, this publication is also intended to serve as an example of creative excellence in design for senior store management, visual merchandising directors, store planners and designers, architects, teachers, and students.

Store interior design is a recognized tool of marketing and an aid to selling goods and services. Hence, this book should contribute to every merchant's ongoing retail education.

We would be remiss if several individuals responsible for the administration of the competition were not recognized: Andre C. Ruellan, I.S.P. international chairman and Steve Duffy, chairman of the I.S.P. Design Contest Committee, both labored for many long hours pulling this sizable program together.

In addition, the winners were selected by leaders in the fields of retail, design, development, and education. Our sincere thanks go to Helen Galland, former president of Bonwit Teller; Joseph Parriott, chairman, the Graduate Department of Industrial Design, Pratt Institute; William Brown, professor of Design, Northern Illinois University, and Dan Morganelli, president, Dan Morganelli Associates, Inc.

Finally, there is a great deal of information provided on the following pages. The ultimate use of this material is up to you. The publication of this book does not however, constitute an express or implied endorsement by the National Retail Merchants Association (NRMA), or the Institute of Store Planners (ISP), of any particular product, service, or firm.

John A. Murphy, Vice President,
NATIONAL RETAIL MERCHANTS ASSOCIATION

Jill Von Schlanbusch, International President,
INSTITUTE OF STORE PLANNERS

New Full Line Department Stores

Bloomingdale's
Miami, Florida

Macy's
Miami, Florida

Burdines
Gainesville, Florida

The new full line department store is often a new location of an existing chain of stores; sometimes it is the first unit of a chain in a particular area.

This places additional burdens on the designers. First, the store must compare favorably with other locations of the same chain. If customers are familiar with the chain's other locations, it's likely that the chain will want new units to reflect the feeling, if not the actual visual style, of existing stores. Customers already familiar with the chain's other locations should feel the new unit is on an equal level, in terms of design and luxury of decoration, as the previous stores.

Second, the new unit should compare favorably with rival department stores in the area to help foster shopper loyalty.

Third, the new unit should establish a strong image. While maintaining the style of the chain's other locations, the design should also make whatever changes are necessary to adapt the store to the area in which it's located.

It's interesting to note that two of the three winners in this category are Miami, Florida branches of old, established New York City department stores (the third is part of a chain that has been in Florida for many years). Both Macy's and Bloomingdale's have very definitive images on their own turf, and would be expected to maintain those images in their new locations. However, New York is not Miami, either in climate or clientele. The urban locations of the flagship stores in both chains gives way, in Miami, to the surburban mall.

The design of these stores, therefore, had to be tailored not only to a different kind of physical configuration, the mall's sprawling layout on a few levels as opposed to the vertical box dictated by Manhattan's incredible real estate costs, but to the tastes, previous experience, and expectations of a whole new clientele. Color, in particular, as well as store layout and choice of construction and decorative materials are important.

Aside from visual and structural considerations, the new store must be designed to properly display and merchandise the goods appropriate to this new clientele. The new location is not a clone of the original either in its physical presentation or in its marketing concept.

For example, the store which was chosen as the best single design of the year, the Bloomingdale's at The Falls shopping center in Miami is what designer Jim Terrell describes as "a new generation of stores." In contrast to the rather small, enclosed spaces of earlier Bloomingdale's, the new store features open vistas and well-organized traffic flow which allows the shopper to know where he or she is at all times, making the store easier to shop. The open, atrium-like escalator well, enclosed in glass and topped with a skylight, adds to the shopper's sense of location, assisted by the strong axial lines of the aisles between departments.

The typical Bloomingdale's style gives way to local variation in the use of color. At "The Falls," a soft, muted, "tropical" palette replaces the strong, graphic hues of other stores in the chain. Yet despite all these changes, the store is unmistakeably Bloomingdale's.

The Macy's in Miami, which took honorable mention, has as its goal something more than opening another branch in a different part of the country. With its high-style look—a romantic, curved design of unusual fluidity, free-flowing curved aisles, stainless steel columns and marble floors—the store actually has people lining up to get in each morning. More than a tourist attraction, the Miami store also represents Macy's first venture into serving an upper-class market; a serious bid for shoppers a little more affluent than the predominantly lower-middle class clientele which are the mainstay of its New York City location. This puts Macy's head to head for the to the same upper middle-class shoppers currently served by Bloomingdale's. The explosive population growth and corresponding rise in affluence in the Miami area make it an almost ideal market for this type of upward mobility.

Bloomingdale's

The Falls
Miami, Florida

Designed by: Hambrecht Terrell International
New York, New York

Store Of The Year
First Award, New Full Line Department Stores

This Bloomingdale's, the chain's first unit in Florida, marks a departure from previous designs. As a prototype for future Bloomingdale's, it should serve admirably, having won the highest award given by designers to new stores:
The Store of the Year.

Spatially, Bloomingdale's have traditionally been enclosed spaces with narrow penetrations and deep departments. At The Falls, the departments were made narrow and wide, bringing more merchandise close to the aisles. Wide, clear spaces were left between departments to provide graceful and effective transitions.

The materials were chosen to reflect the Bloomingdale's lifestyle: marble, bleached teak, chrome. Contemporary without being self-conscious, the furnishings provide a flexible and dramatic backdrop for the merchandise.

The design is thoroughly contemporary in its use of color. Beige, pink, and mint green predominate, warming the interior with a soft color palette appropriate to the sensibilities of today's shopper and effective in showcasing the fashionable goods the store is known for.

Project: Bloomingdale's "The Falls"
Location: Miami, Florida
Client: Bloomingdale's, New York, New York
Design Firm: Hambrecht Terrell International
New York, New York

This is the first Bloomingdale's in Florida. This 225,000-square-foot facility represents a significant departure from other Bloomingdale's. In order to capture a feeling of openness and light, a three-story central atrium was created. Visual merchandise displays are cantilevered into the atrium from the second floor, and a bridge passes over the atrium on the third floor.

INTERIOR DESIGN TEAM

Planners:	James E. Terrell, John Czorny
Designers:	James E. Terrell, Martin Jerry, Wyatt Neal
Decorator:	Debra M. Robusto
Job Captain:	Waldo Sarjeant
Project Manager:	John Czorny
Partners in charge:	John Czorny, James E. Terrell
President/chairmen:	James E. Terrell, Edward C. Hambrecht
Consultant:	David A. Mintz (lighting)
Contractors:	Amertec Granada, Goebel Fixtures, Acme Fixture Co., Crown Store Equipment

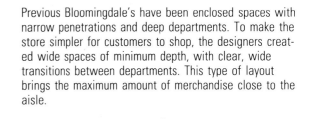

Previous Bloomingdale's have been enclosed spaces with narrow penetrations and deep departments. To make the store simpler for customers to shop, the designers created wide spaces of minimum depth, with clear, wide transitions between departments. This type of layout brings the maximum amount of merchandise close to the aisle.

First-floor plan: The atrium serves as both a central focal point and as a way for customers to easily orient themselves while shopping. A simple circulation pattern was developed, emphasizing a perimeter loop with axial cross aisles converging at the atrium.

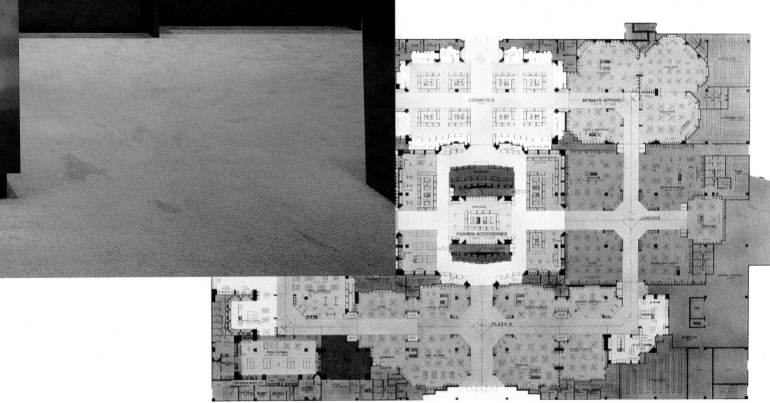

Materials were chosen for durability and for their appropriateness in portraying the Bloomingdale's lifestyle. Marble and bleached teak form all aisles, and are arranged in patterns which complement the store's visual merchandising.

The emphasis on careful integration of both materials and colors is evident. Looking from the cosmetics area into Men's World, the eye is caressed by a comforting blend of beige, warm pink, and mint green. Coordinated accents are provided by tinted glass dividers between the departments, plants, a mint green stripe around a step in the multi-tiered ceiling, a pot of coleus on the counter, and irridescent planters atop the islands. Pink and black Bloomingdale's bags were designed for the department and are used to enhance the decor.

The sense of enveloping brightness so typical of Florida landscapes is brought indoors through use of a mixture of incandescent spot and fluorescent trough lighting. Merchandised full-height walls are washed with light, and the merchandise is highlighted, without creating dark spots.

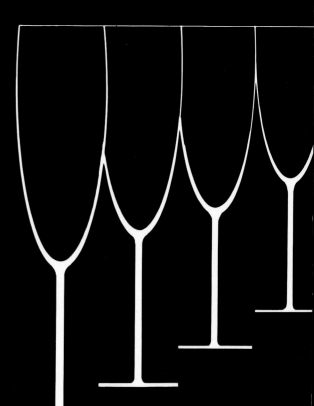

Broad vistas play against dramatic visual merchandise displays at the intersection of all aisles.

Wood and glass screens give the departments a sense
of enclosure without blocking the view into other areas.

Second-floor plan: Fashion merchandise is concentrated
on the first two levels with housewares taking part
of level two and all of level three.

The soft, warm colors and materials used throughout are a marked contrast to previous Bloomingdale's. The varied wall treatments provide dramatic, yet flexible, backgrounds for the display of merchandise.

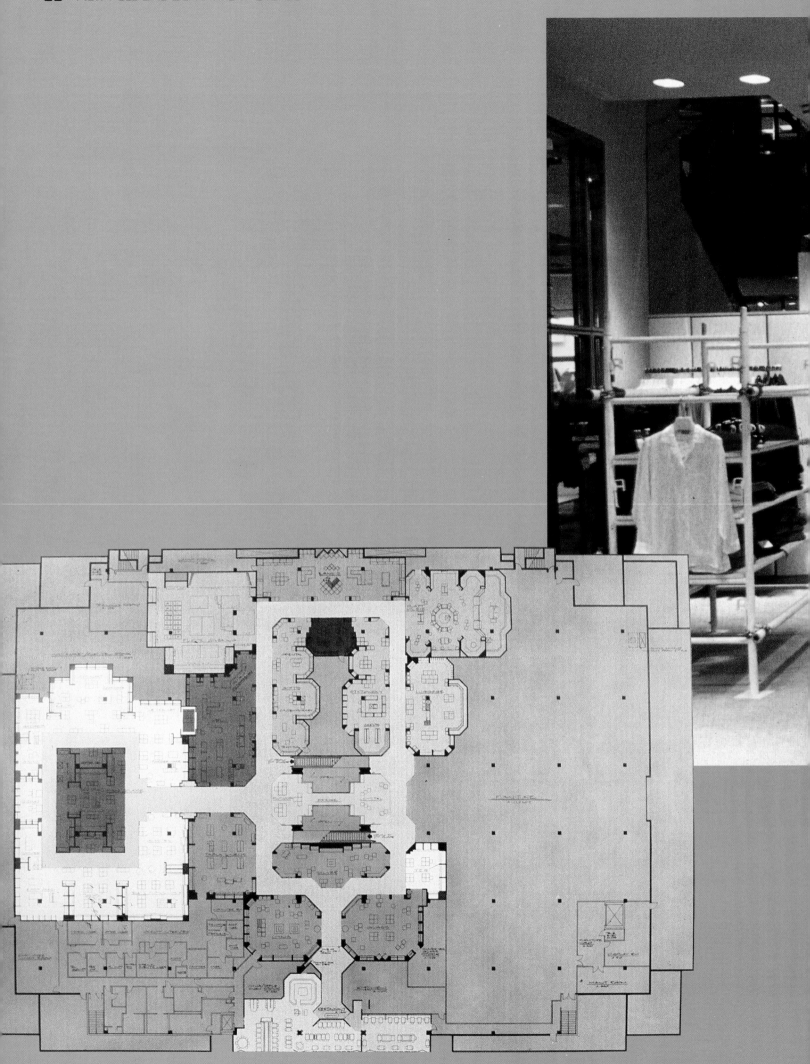

Third-floor plan: This store, with its feeling of space and light, will be a prototype for the next generation of Bloomingdale's stores.

Though materials in the specialty departments are varied, the thematic colors and lighting are carried through. This consistency contributes to the shopper's identification with the store.

Macy's

Aventura Mall
North Miami, Florida

Designed by: CNI International
New York, New York

Honorable Mention, New Full Line Department Stores

A large store, the Macy's in North Miami is spread over 282,000 square feet on three separate levels. The entire store was themed to a series of curvilinear planes, and organized around a spectacular escalator bank at the center of the traffic pattern.

The planes start at the perimeter of the departments, where the ceilings are dropped, and build toward the center. Aisle ceilings soar above the departments, repeating the planes and rising toward the rotunda above the escalator bank.

The interior was calculated to show a family resemblence to the parent store in New York, but with a Floridian flair. Lively pastel colors were introduced into the design scheme and the repetitive use of curves suggests a certain informality appropriate to the tropics.

Project: Macy's Aventura Mall
Location: North Miami, Florida
Client: R.H. Macy, Inc.
New York, New York
Design Firm: CNI International
New York, New York

Luxurious design elements—marble, wood veneer, stainless steel, decorative wall coverings—set a contemporary tone. The palette of colors chosen for the store reflects its location in sub-tropical Florida.

INTERIOR DESIGN TEAM

Planner:	Gale Barter
Designer:	Tom Tarnowski
Decorator:	Patty Madden
Project Manager:	Charles Arato
Partner in charge:	Bernhart H. Rumphorst
President/chairman:	Lawrence Israel
Contractors:	HBSA/Amertec, Crafted Cabinet Beacon

Spread over 282,000 square feet on three levels, this Macy's in North Miami, Florida was designed to reflect the style of the parent store in New York, but with a Floridian flair.

A spectacular escalator bank serves as the central vertical spine and the focal point of the entire store. Visually, the escalators repeat the interior architectural theme of curvilinear planes, which culminates in the rotunda over the escalator shaft.

Each individual department was given a highly distinctive visual character. While each shopping "world" is unique, they share a common architectural theme. Variations in ceiling height are echoed by curvilinear planes in coves and enframements and are reflected in the design of showcases. The result is a series of concentric planes rising from the perimeter of the store to the center of the rotunda.

The circular traffic aisle system revolves around the escalators. The architecture, design and use of materials helps guide shoppers, inviting them to explore all areas of the huge space. Even though the departments are highly stylized and individual, transitions between departments are smooth and flowing.

Marble floor aisles flow past the women's departments creating a luxurious design element.

The colors and finishes used in the cosmetics department—marble columns in the men's areas, and lacquered pastels in the women's areas— provide a luxurious background for the merchandise.
◄

The entranceway to the Children's World department is wide and spacious. White neon lights set a contemporary tone. ►

Burdines

Oaks Mall
Gainesville, Florida

Designed by: Walker/Group Inc.
New York, New York

Honorable Mention, New Full Line Department Stores

The design for this Burdines in Gainesville, Florida is more than a bit whimsical. Kenneth Walker, head of the firm which designed the facility, says he likes to select elements that reflect the unique locale of each store.

The Brobdingnagian alligator columns—each 35 feet tall—surrounding the escalator core are certainly unique. They are appropriate to the locale, as well. Gainesville is the location of the University of Florida, whose mascot is the alligator.

The other imperatives for this location were to be as contemporary as possible. The area is dominated by young, educated, affluent, style-conscious shoppers.

Dramatic department settings, bold merchandise displays, and heavy use of neon signs help underscore this commitment to the present. This commitment is visible from the parking lot; in contrast to the beige brick veneer used on other stores in the mall, the exterior was faced with aluminum panels with turquoise and pink reveals. These colors are continued throughout the store, tying its diverse elements together with a uniform, overscale trim.

Project: Burdines, Gainesville
Location: Oaks Mall, Gainesville, Florida
Client: Burdines, Miami, Florida
Owner: Federated Department Stores, Cincinnati, Ohio
Design Firm: Walker/Group, Inc.

This new Burdines in Gainesville, Florida was designed to appeal to the area's young, style-conscious shoppers.

Sculpted columns resembling alligators add to the impression of height and firmly root this store in its locale: The mascot of the University of Florida, located in Gainesville, is the alligator.

INTERIOR DESIGN TEAM

Design Team	Masado Endo, Florence Orlando, Steve Kitzeh, Sherrie Zwail, Susan Long, Greg Tice
Project Coordinator:	Errol Spence
Project Manager:	Franco Iampieri
Partner in charge:	Raul Nunez
Lighting:	Walker/Group, Inc.
Building Architects:	Reynolds Smith & Hills
Perimeter:	Anton Waldman Associates
Loose fixtures:	American Woodcraft, Inc.
Showcase:	Goer Manufacturing Co.
Back Island:	Wood Wizards, Inc.
Mechanical/Electr. Eng:	H.J. Ross & Associates
Sculptured columns:	Zafero Studio
Sculptor:	Juan Segura

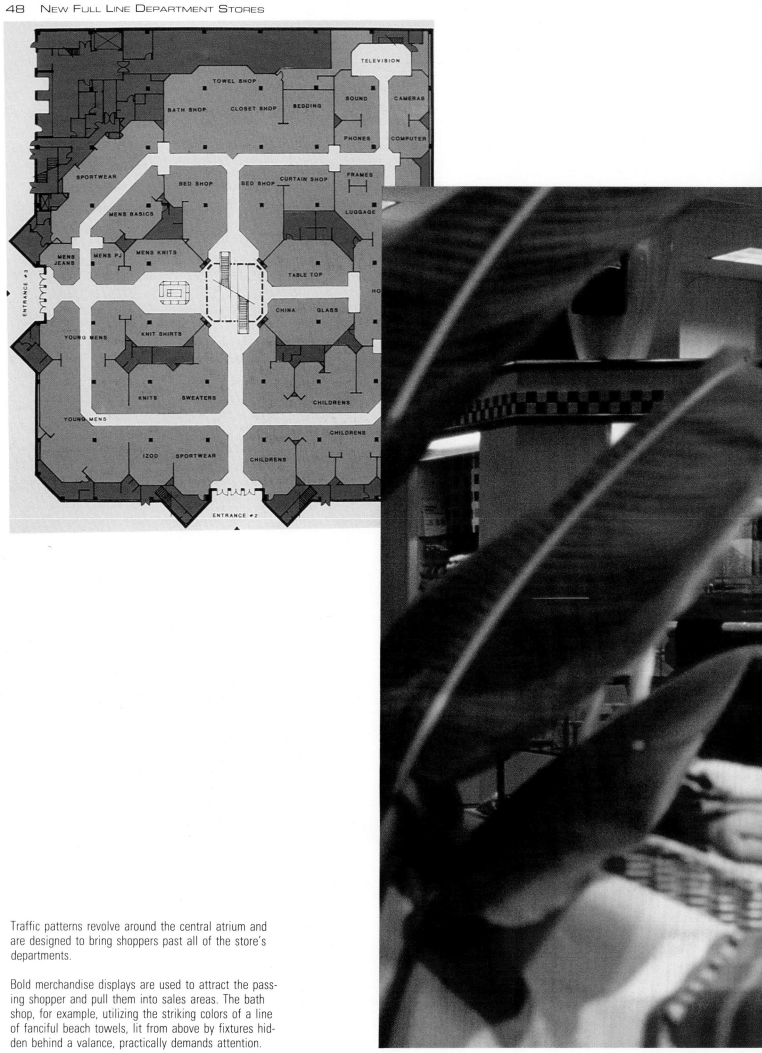

Traffic patterns revolve around the central atrium and are designed to bring shoppers past all of the store's departments.

Bold merchandise displays are used to attract the passing shopper and pull them into sales areas. The bath shop, for example, utilizing the striking colors of a line of fanciful beach towels, lit from above by fixtures hidden behind a valance, practically demands attention.

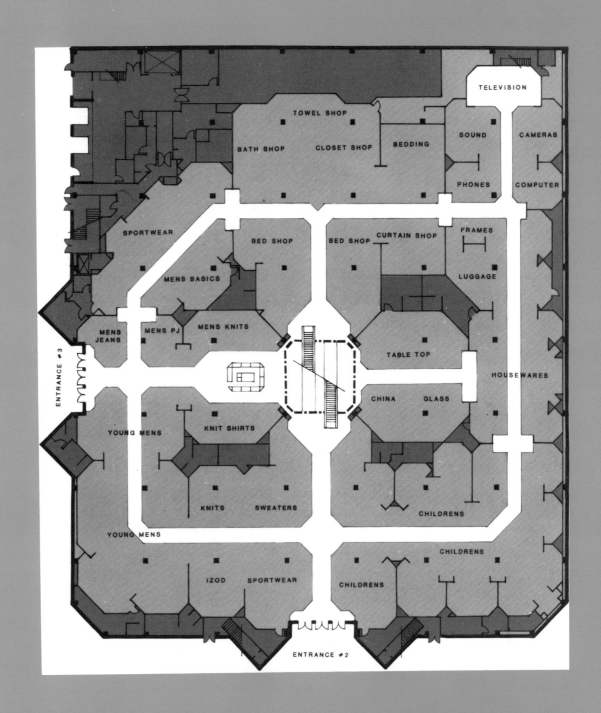

Large feature display areas are designed into each department, and walls provide additional feature displays. Low wall sections allow shoppers to see beyond the immediate department in some areas.

An atrium with a 35-foot high skylight at the center of the store acts as an architectural spine and an orientation device. Diffused sunlight floods the core, adding to the sense of spaciousness.

MALL ENTRANCE

SPORTSWEAR

SPORTSWEAR

SPORTSWEAR

SPORTSWEAR

SPORTSWEAR

SPORTSWEAR

TOP SHOP

SPORTSWEAR

SPORTSWEAR

WOMENS SHOES

SPORTSWEAR

JUNIORS

JUNIORS

COSMETICS

ENTRANCE #1

JUNIORS

DRESSES

DRESSES

LOUNGEWEAR

SLEEPWEAR

DRESSES

FOUNDATIONS

Materials and design concepts are used thematically throughout the women's area using half-round moldings placed vertically; placed horizontally in strips in the men's and atrium areas; and grouped together in the juniors area.

Department names also carry out the local sports imagery. Alligator Alley is the name of the original basketball facility at the University of Florida. This whimsical approach to decor is followed up throughout the store. During football season, the atrium alligators are decorated whenever the team wins, and during Christmas, they're clothed in Santa Claus suits.

Looking from women's sportswear, past the atrium and on toward the dress department, the pink and turquoise theme is continued through the use of pink walls and ceilings and an overscale turquoise trim.

RENOVATED FULL LINE DEPARTMENT STORES

Carson, Pirie, Scott
Mount Prospect, Illinois

Macy's
Monterey, California

The renovation of a full store calls for a number of decisions. How deep will the changes go? Will they be cosmetic, without major construction, or will they involve structural changes to the building?

The answers may be dictated not only to the budget for a renovation, but by the purpose: is the store being given a cosmetic facelift, or are the changes designed to change the marketing thrust of the location?

In renovating the Carson, Pirie, Scott store in Mount Prospect, Illinois, designer Steve Duffy decided to make the renovated store vastly different from the original. The store was given a strong architectural shape, including a strong ceiling featuring dark gray steps against white, and dramatic views of the aisles.

The need for unity in this store, which sells everything from glassware to men's wear, is satisfied by design elements which are repeated in the diverse departments. Although these design elements are consistent, the store's various merchandise "worlds" are clearly defined by a straight aisle pattern that provides a clearly engineered traffic flow through what is essentially a type of "mini-mall."

The mall entrance is located in a corner of the store's middle level, which is primarily devoted to women's fashions. A ring-road aisle system floored in peach-colored tiles begins at the entrance, and brings shoppers past the perimeter departments and through a central mall to the escalators which provide access to the upper and lower levels.

The renovated store's basic color theme is peach, rose, and beige, with individual departments given differently colored accents. The juniors department, for example, is highlighted with charcoal carpet and fixtures, while the men's department is done in taupe and brown.

Carson, Pirie, Scott's decision to renovate clearly reflects demographic and lifestyle changes in the store's market area. A continuing trend toward greater affluence among the department store's most economically significant customers—young professional singles and couples—have created a movement toward more high-style and high-line merchandise. To properly showcase this upscale merchandise and please the upscale consumer requires a store with an "upscale" appearance. More highly stylized interiors and a greater use of "luxury" building materials are two manifestations of this trend. Both of these techniques were used in the Carson, Pirie, Scott renovation.

The new look in stores, evidenced both in new buildings and renovations, is one of space and directness. The need to make a store easy to shop is frequently reiterated by designers. As department stores continue to cut back on their sales personnel, with fewer staff available to advise or direct, this need becomes more acute. Straight aisles, strong sightlines and easily-identified departments become important.

High-tech decor remains a significant current in contemporary store design, as is evidenced in the Macy's store in Monterey, California.

While Carson, Pirie, Scott's renovation was dictated by the need to respond to a changing clientele, the renovation of the Macy's in Monterey, California, was undertaken to gain more selling space and provide a facelift for the store.

To gain the additional space for this two-level suburban mall store, a below-ground parking area was converted into a sales area. Escalators lead from the main floor down to a concourse in the former parking area.

The lower-level concourse is L-shaped and is floored with ceramic tile. Modular glass and metal storefronts flank the concourse, providing show window and shop entries for the Housewares and Domestics departments. These ultra-contemporary accents update the aging facility's appearance, as well as provide strong identification for the individual departments.

Carson, Pirie, Scott

Randhurst Shopping Center,
Mount Prospect, Illinois

Designed by: CNI International
New York, New York

Honorable Mention, Renovated Full Line Department Stores

CNI International's renovation for Carson, Pirie, Scott had to satisfy a number of needs. The existing facility was 22 years old, and the company wanted to introduce a number of new departments and eliminate others.

The solution was to create mini-malls containing a series of specialty shops defined by beam drops. These areas were set apart architecturally, yet had to be open enough to encourage browsing so as not to hinder customer service.

The existing interior was out of tune with the changed lifestyle of its shoppers, so locations were needed for new types of businesses. The decorations were to be made more contemporary and appropriate to the new customer.

A varied color palette was chosen, with colors themed to major sales areas. Men's World was done in brown and taupe, while Home World was executed in shades of gray. Within the major merchandise groupings, individual departments were given their own thematic colors, as well.

Project: Carson, Pirie, Scott
Location: Randhurst Shopping Center,
Mount Prospect, Illinois
Client: Carson, Pirie, Scott & Company

Renovations to the 22-year-old Carson, Pirie, Scott store at the Randhurst Shopping Center outside of Chicago were undertaken to introduce new departments, change the ambiance to fit the evolving psychographics of the clientele, and to completely re-engineer traffic flow in the three-level facility.

INTERIOR DESIGN TEAM

Planner: Frank Sluzas
Designer: Frank Sullivan
Decorator: Catherine Murray
Job Captain: Tom Harvin
Partner in charge: Andre Ruellan
Contractors: Bernhardt Store Fixture Co. (fixtures)
Pritcher & Erbach (general contractor)

The mall entrance is located in a corner of the store's middle level. A ring-road aisle system floored in peach-colored tiles begins at the entrance, and brings shoppers past the perimeter departments and through a central mall to the escalators which provide access to the upper and lower levels.

The new layout was conceived as a series of mini-malls, specialty departments. These were to be well-defined by variations in ceiling, dividers, and other interior details, yet open enough to encourage browsing and facilitate customer service.

SHESEIDO

Ceiling and floor displays define the two separate areas on this level. Brown and taupe were used in Men's World, while medium gray and lavender gray were used in the home section.

Within the peach/rose/beige color scheme, individual departments are given their own definitive accents. The Juniors department is highlighted with charcoal gray carpet and fixtures.

The 17,000-square-foot lower level was divided into two areas, Men's World and Home World. The escalator down deposits shoppers at the plaza entrance to Men's World, and the return is by an escalator in the plaza of Home World. An additional plaza was created to draw attention to the extension at the end of the Decorative Home Center core aisle.

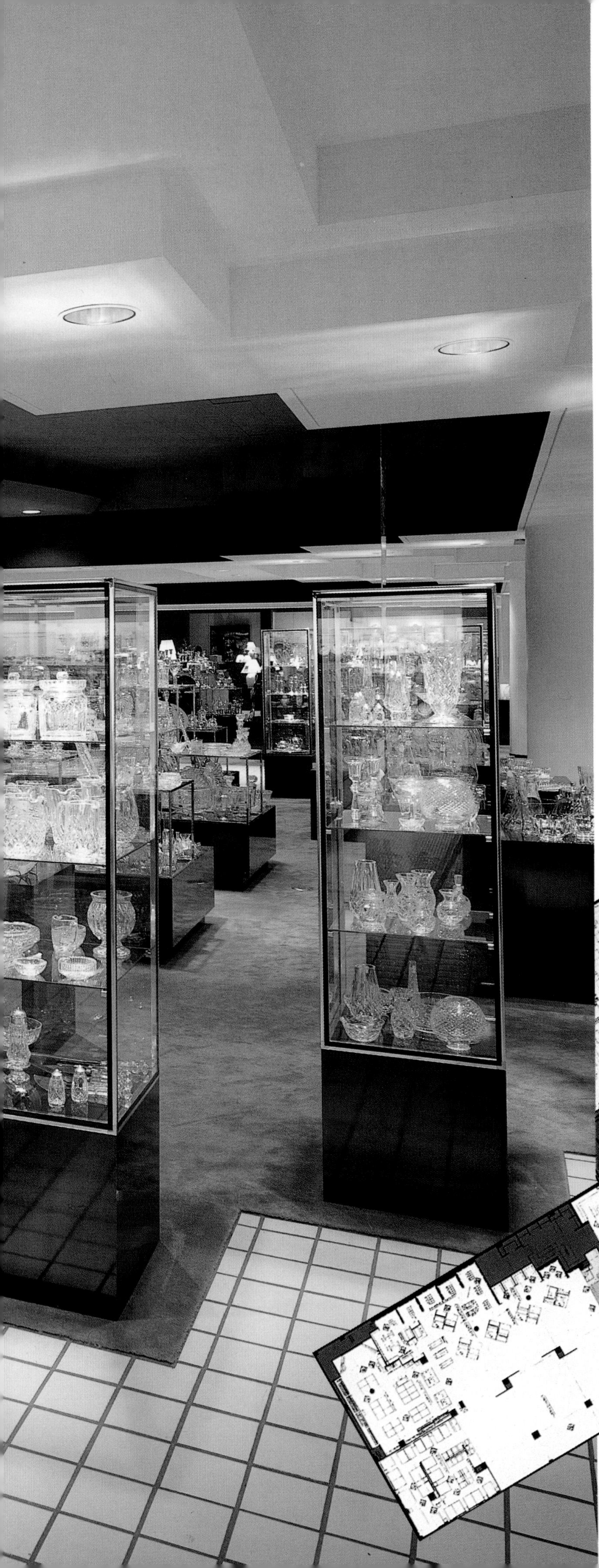

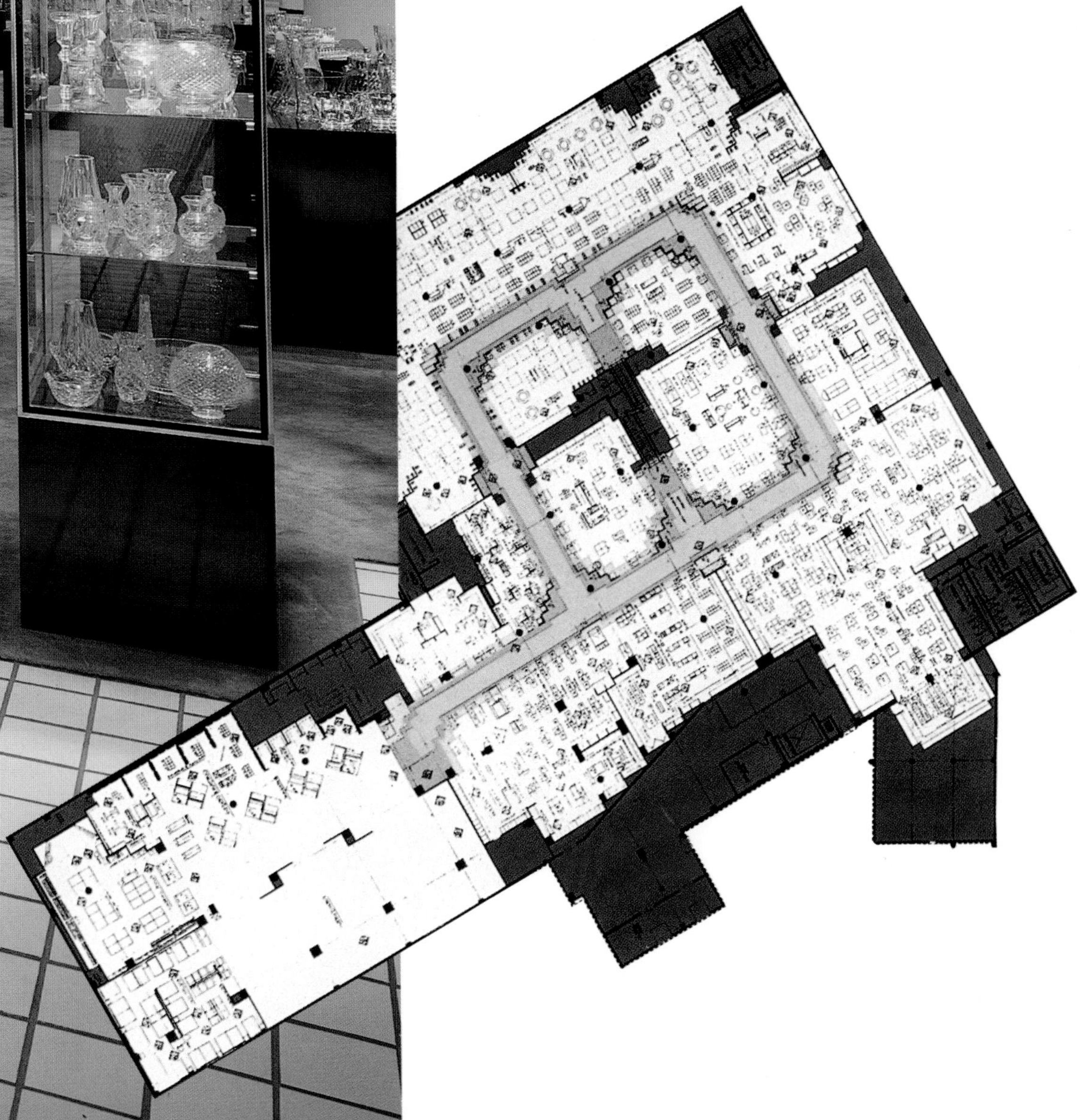

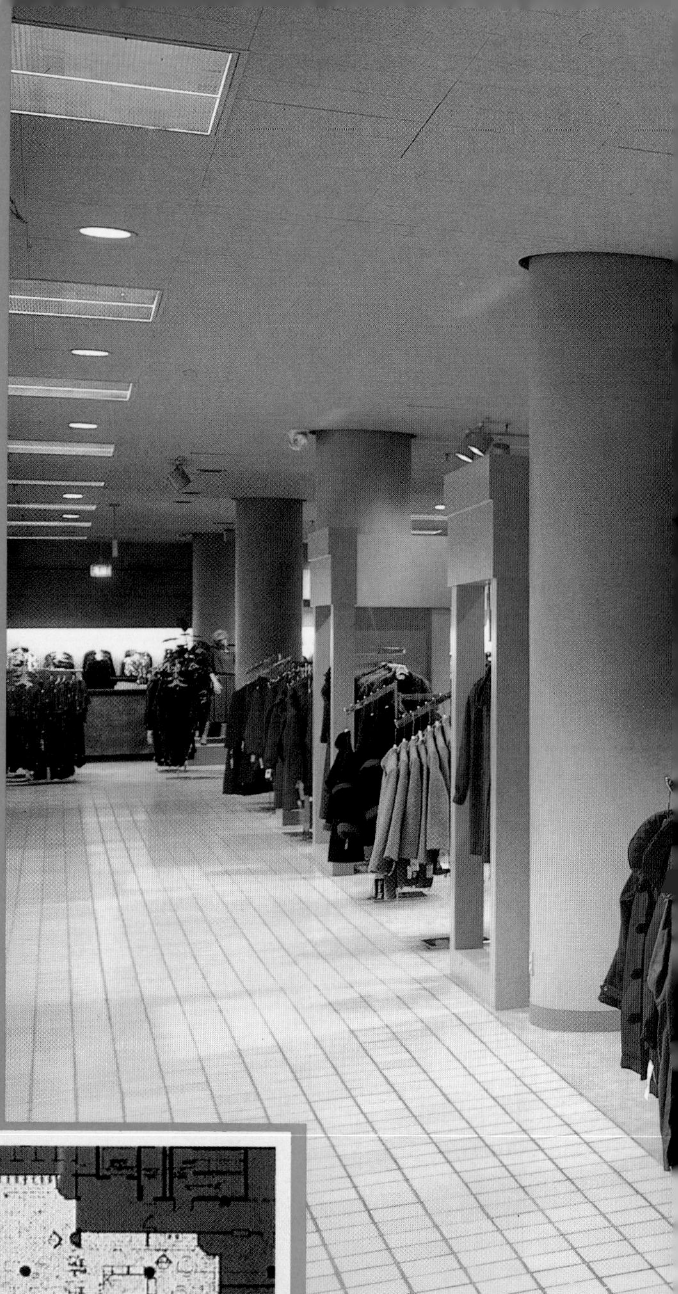

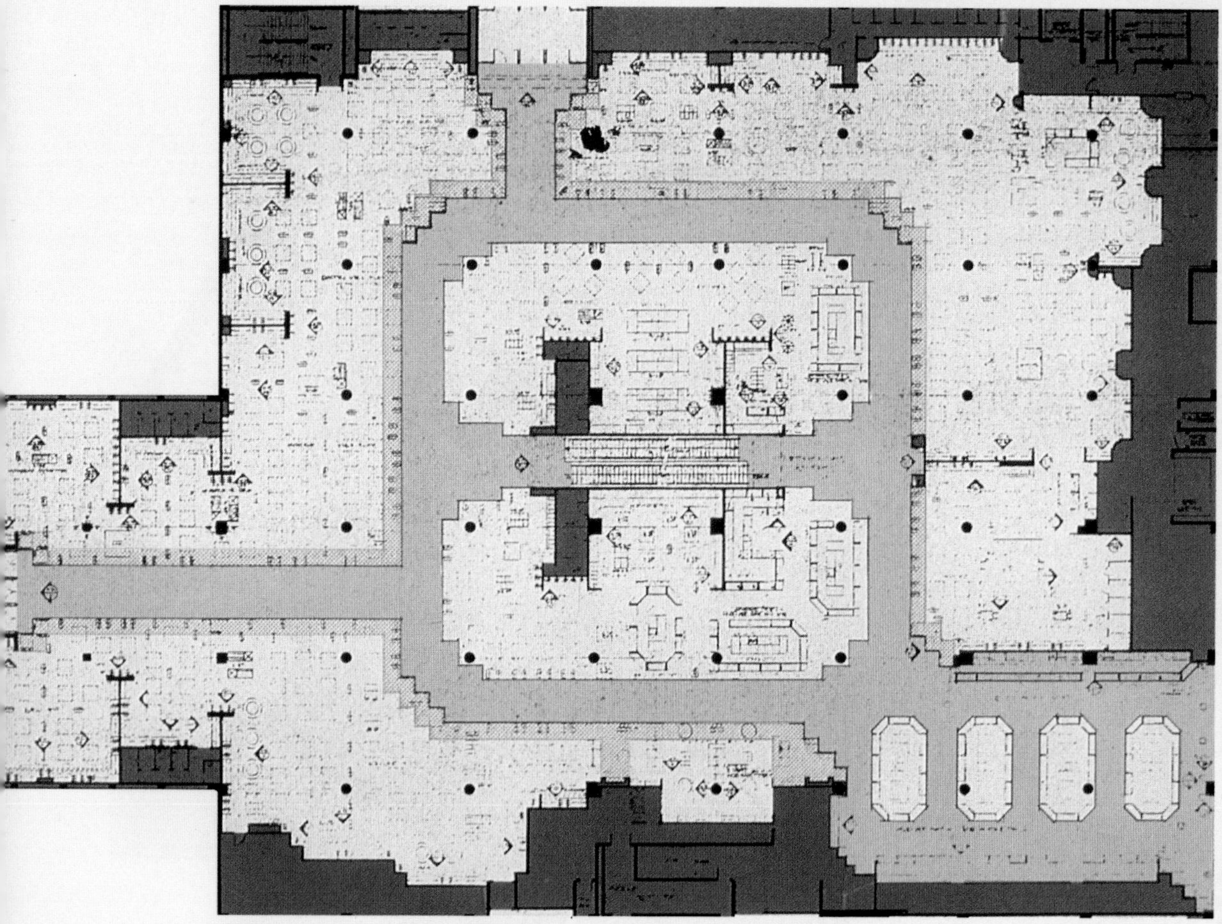

The accent of the middle level is on women's fashions. The color tones are subtle variations of salmon, beige, and rose. The aisle from the mall entrance leads directly past the cosmetics area before passing the clothing and accessories areas.

The escalator up from the middle level brings customers into a department themed for the corporate woman. Open plan dividers and architectural black dividers create a different atmosphere in this area, yet the aisle system gracefully moves past the corporate department into Women's Ready-to-Wear, themed in salmon and deep rose; Intimate Apparel, in sunset rose and soft pink; and Children's World, decorated in shades of lavender.

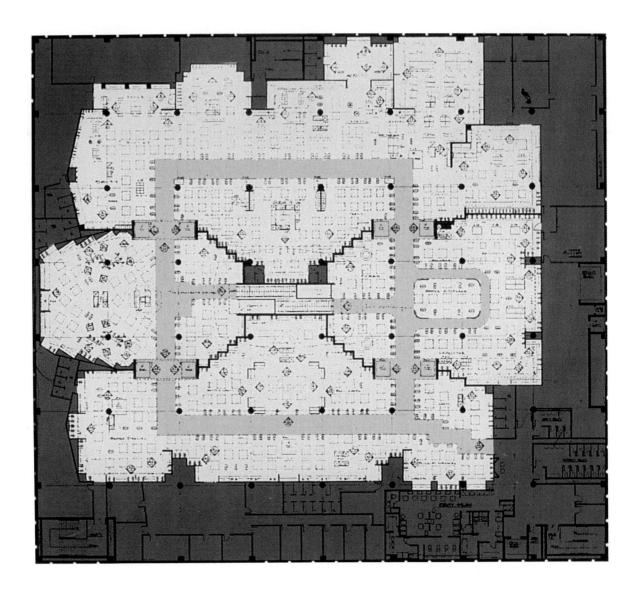

Macy's

Del Monte Shopping Center
Monterey, California

Designed by: Store Planning Associates
San Francisco, California

Honorable Mention, Renovated Full Line Department Stores

Renovating an existing space poses special design problems. To acquire more selling space, Macy's converted a below-grade garage from parking space to sales floor.

This new lower level features an L-shaped concourse floored with ceramic tile. Modular metal-framed display windows project into the passageway, reinforcing the store's layout as a series of retail boutiques. Metal-framed doorways lead into the housewares and domestics departments.

Escalators from the concourse level deliver shoppers to a first-floor pavillion, also accented with the metal framing.

Color is used extensively to identify departments and guide shoppers. While the electronics area is dark gray, a department devoted to table top items just opposite to it is done in a subdued salmon. The final core element of the main floor is Children's world, where turquoise is used for the girls department, bright red for boys, and peach for infants and toddlers.

Project: Macy's
Location: Del Monte Shopping Center
Monterey, California
Client: R. H. Macy, Inc.
New York, New York

In order to gain additional selling space for this two-level suburban mall store, a below-ground parking area was converted into a sales area. Escalators lead from the main floor down to a concourse in the former parking area.

INTERIOR DESIGN TEAM

Planner:	Buz Pierpoint
Designers:	Don Lipp, Ilana Griswold
Decorator:	Ilana Griswold
Job Captain:	Betty Collins
Partner in charge:	Buz Pierpoint
President/Chairman:	Robert L. Huck
Contractors:	Valley Showcase, Custom Craft Fixtures, Images Woodworking, Zimmerla Corp., Acme Cabinet Co.

Aisles create a strong flow from the four mall entrances to a central plaza. The plaza is dominated by a Jewelry and Accessory area furnished in brushed brass and marble.

◄

The lower-level concourse is L-shaped and is floored with ceramic tile. Modular glass and metal storefronts flank the concourse, providing show window and shop entries for the Housewares and Domestics departments.

The interior of the Children's World department on the lower level is distinguished by color divisions: red for boys, dark turquoise for girls, and peach for infants. The areas are tied together through the use of white accents and white neon lights.

Wood flooring and carpet, textured plaster, and natural wood millwork create a casual atmosphere in the Domestics department on the lower level.

This women's-wear department was designed to appeal to young, style-conscious shoppers.

Glass showcases highlight displays between the men's and women's department.

Soft Goods Specialty Stores

Burdines
Coconut Grove, Florida

L.L.Bean
Freeport, Maine

Parisian
Huntsville, Alabama

Soft goods specialty stores, while carrying a more limited line of goods, still must satisfy many of the same consumer demands as full line department stores. As a result, their marketing, as reflected in the store design, is similar as well. Functionally, this means a movement toward more open space, generally to straighter aisles, and toward the inclusion of emphasis on upscale merchandise.

In renovating or building new stores for chains, designers are often constrained by the need for consistency from one location to another. This is difficult enough given the normal variations between units. But the designers of the Burdines in the Mayfair-in-the-Grove had an especially difficult challenge. The chain's other area locations are full line department stores, most located in sprawling suburban malls. The Mayfair store, in the densely-populated Coconut Grove section of Miami, Florida, carries a much more limited selection of merchandise. The product mix is geared to upper-class, international consumers, rather than to middle-class residents, as are other Burdines. Additionally, the mall itself provides no large rectangles for its tenants, so that the space occupied by Burdines is very narrow and elongated.

While only 70,000 square feet, the store is spread over three levels, challenging the designers to create an effective traffic flow to carry shoppers through and between departments. Their solution was to use a very strong axial spline to move consumers past departments separated with glass partitions, which define selling areas without obstructing sightlines or visually reducing the already limited space.

Consistency among locations was not a consideration in the renovation of the L. L. Bean retail store. The famous catalog merchandiser operates but one facility, located in Freeport, Maine.

The renovation was prompted by Bean's need to slow inventory turns and provide more display space in the store, which is open 24 hours a day, seven days a week.

A two-story addition was constructed and connected to the existing three-story building, almost doubling the total selling area to 60,000 square feet. Custom wood and glass fixtures were designed to accommodate Bean's merchandise, with the bins, shelves, and dividers calculated to hold exactly the right proportion of products and sizes in each department.

In the sales areas, the company's colors, brown and deep green, were used in signage to provide a familiar element for shoppers and to reinforce Bean's identity.

All of these trends are reflected in Schaefer Associates' design for Parisian, in Huntsville, Alabama.

Before designing the store, the designers first conducted a thorough marketing study of the community. What they found, according to designer Charles Sparks, was a community of great contrast.

While Huntsville's business community is decidedly modern, the marketing study also found a great respect for the area's history—an attitude firmly embedded in the culture of the rural South.

The designers attempted to express this contrast in the design of the store. A central plaza was created, with a "sensate zone" consisting of one level for gourmet foods and another, slightly lower level for fragrances. The open space above the plaza features balconies and strong sightlines for people-watching and is illuminated by a clerestory window. This modern treatment is softened by the use of neo-Gothic architectural accents on the two-story walls of the central plaza. These accents, while given a crisp, modern look, vividly recall the columns, porticos, and peaked roofs of the area's 19th-century mansions.

This "Parisian Plaza" became a marketing tool for the store, providing space for fashion shows and other special events and promotionals.

The store also incorporates some high-tech elements. An electronic showboard at the store's entrance consisting of 12 high-resolution TV monitors is used to display videos from video discs players. When special events such as fashion shows or food preparation exhibitions are being conducted in the store, they are simultaneously shown on these screens.

Parisian's design differs from other contemporary store designs in two significant ways. While there is a strong organization and thoughtful flow provided by the floor plan, the aisles were not laid out with long, uninterrupted straight sections. The traffic plan provides easy flow throughout the store, exposing shoppers to all departments. The aisles are shaped into shorter segments to encourage easy circulation and provide more exposure along the aisles for merchandise. Best-of-class merchandise is located at critical circulation points, such as the entryways and bends in aisles.

The second difference is in the ceiling treatment. Unlike many other new stores and renovations, Parisian employs a ceiling of a single height to give an impression of unity. Also, the ceiling is tinted a darker color to keep customers' eyes down on the merchandise and on the aisles. The need to differentiate departments is served through the use of dividers and signage.

Burdines

Mayfair-In-The-Grove
Coconut Grove, Florida

Designed by: Walker/Group Inc.
New York, New York

First Award, Soft Goods Specialty Stores

An affluent area of Miami, Coconut Grove concentrates all of the cosmopolitan verve and international connections of this port city. The design challenge was to use an unusual existing space to create a store for upscale, international consumers.

The mall itself is unusual, even in a city filled with experimental and non-traditional architecture. The multi-level building faced with rough-textured concrete surrounds a central courtyard filled with plants and open to the elements.

As a consequence of the mall's design, Burdines' retail space is long and narrow, with 70,000 square feet spread over three levels. Also, the connections to the mall and a future hotel were predetermined and could not be relocated.

A strong axial spline was created to tie the space together. On the first two levels, a row of regularly-spaced columns lines one side of this major aisle, and glass partitions were used to divide the area into departments without closing it in. In keeping with the affluence of the mall's clientele, rich materials such as marble, ceramic tile, and fabrics were used to impart a rich, almost residential, ambiance.

Project: Burdines
Location: Mayfair-in-the-Grove Shopping Center, Coconut Grove, Florida
Client: Burdines, Miami, Florida
Owner: Federated Department Stores, Cincinnati, Ohio

Designers of the Burdines in the Mayfair-in-the-Grove were challenged by an irregular-shaped space and a directive to create a store that would appeal to a very broad, international, and high-end market. Unlike its other area locations, which are department stores, this Burdines is a specialty store, offering a limited selection of merchandise.

INTERIOR DESIGN TEAM

Design Team: Masako Endo, Kevin Rice, Edwin Sierra, Sherrie Zwail
Job Captain: Ed Stand
Project Manager: Anthony LoGrande
Partner in charge: Raul Nunez
President/Chairman: Kenneth H. Walker
Architects: Treister & Cantillo
Contractor: H.J. Ross

The facility is relatively small, 70,000 square feet on three levels. The cosmetics and women's shoe departments show how rich materials, such as marble, ceramic tile, wood, and fabric were used to provide a luxurious background for the merchandise.

SPORTSWEAR

HANDBAGS

SHOES

FASHION ACCESSORIES

COSMETICS

JEWELRY

SPORTSWEAR

A strong axial spline was created to tie the long, narrow space together, and a row of columns line one side of the central passageways of the first two levels while glass partitions define individual departments.

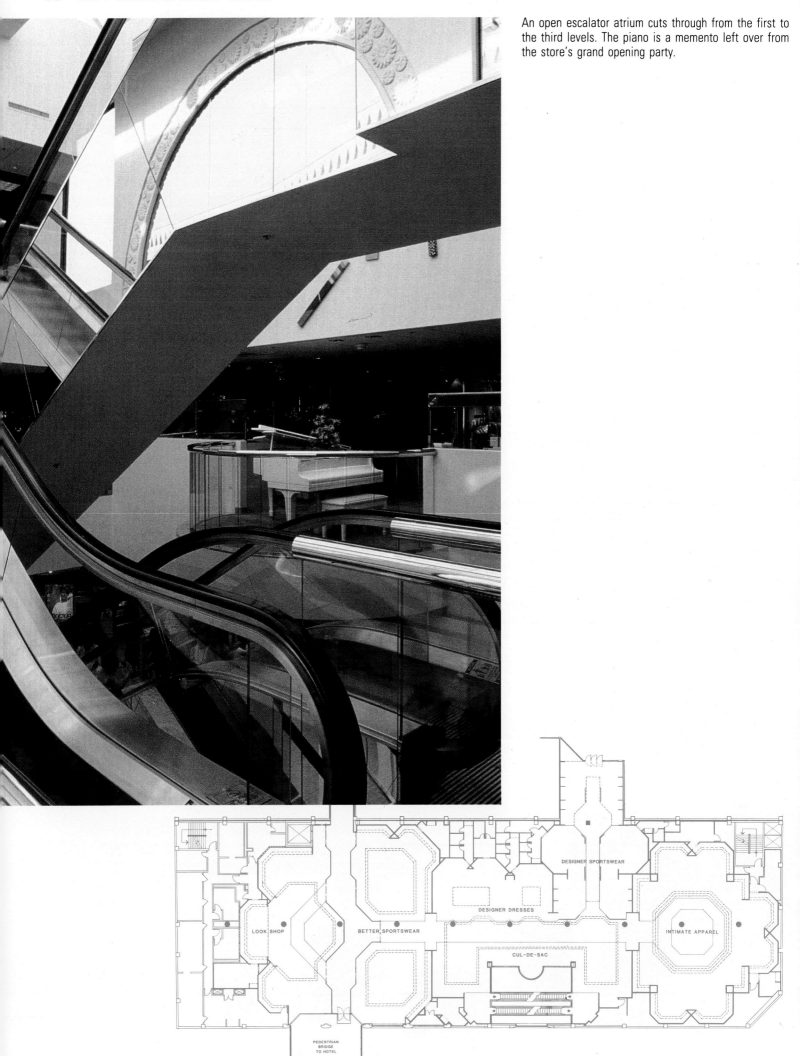

An open escalator atrium cuts through from the first to the third levels. The piano is a memento left over from the store's grand opening party.

LOOK SHOP

BETTER SPORTSWEAR

DESIGNER DRESSES

DESIGNER SPORTSWEAR

INTIMATE APPAREL

CUL-DE-SAC

PEDESTRIAN BRIDGE TO HOTEL

A staggered ceiling is used to differentiate the aisles from the actual selling environments. Ceilings extend to 11 feet above the aisles, but are cut to eight feet within the departments. This makes them more intimate, and the residential feeling is enhanced by the use of mirrored ceilings and columns.

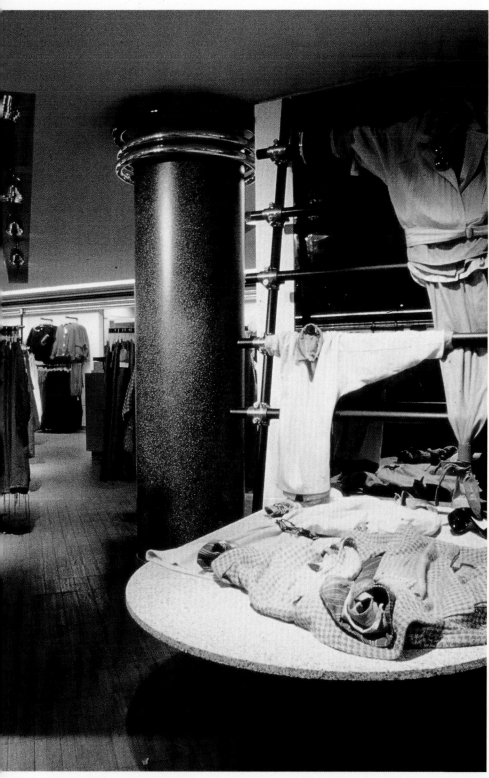

The third level contains a cafe as well as merchandise displays. The custom lighting systems traces the perimeter walls with a baffled light trough containing both fluorescent tubes and an incandescent track system. The colors and finishes of the columns are used as signatures for each department—dark or wood in men's areas, lacquered pastels in the women's areas, and multi-hued pink on the ground floor.

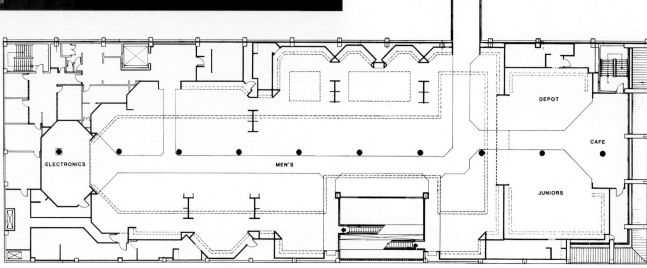

L. L. Bean

Freeport, Maine

Designed by: Retail Planning Associates, Inc.
Columbus, Ohio

Honorable Mention, Soft Goods Specialty Stores

The L.L. Bean retail store was an unusual design challenge. The store is the only retail facility for the giant outdoor apparel and accessories catalog company. The location is open 365 days a year, 24 hours a day, and is something of a local tourist attraction. The company's problem was that stock in the existing store was turning too fast to permit efficient replenishment. This is a store with a shoe department that seats 100, and where customers had to wait for a seat. Some way had to be found to slow turns without sacrificing efficiency or profitability.

A two-story addition was built and connected to the original store, bringing the facility to 60,000 square feet total. This new addition was devoted to soft lines, with men's clothing on the first floor and women's and children's clothing on the second floor. New fixtures were carefully created specifically for Bean, with the planning extending down to the turnover of merchandise by specific items and sizes.

The store has a long tradition and strong following, so the goal was not to impress customers with a new look, but to blend the addition into the Bean "look" so well that shoppers would feel it had been there forever. As a result, the custom fixtures were designed of natural wood, the Bean signature colors of gray and green were used throughout, and signs were hand-lettered to mimic the style of Bean's logo.

Project: L.L. Bean
Location: Freeport, Maine
Owner: L.L. Bean

L.L. Bean, the noted apparel and outdoor accessories catalog retailer owns one retail store, in Freeport, Maine. The facility is open 24 hours a day, seven days a week. Bean needed a larger display space to both accommodate the large number of shoppers visiting the store daily, and to increasing space for stock on display.

INTERIOR DESIGN TEAM

Planner:	John A. Wells
Designer:	John A. Wells
Job Captain:	John A. Wells
Project Manager:	John A. Wells
Partner in charge:	Thomas R. Panek
President:	Michael J. Gade
Consultants:	Symmes, Maini & Associates
Contractor:	Harvey Construction Co., Inc.

A two-story addition was constructed and connected to the existing three-story building, almost doubling the total selling area to 60,000 square feet. The entryway features a skylight and a pond containing live trout. The floor is of granite, and all of the construction materials were chosen to withstand extreme wear.

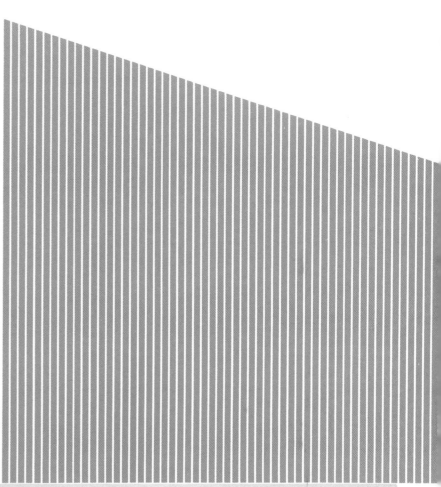

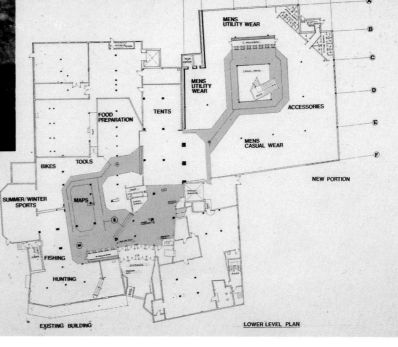

LOWER LEVEL PLAN

Part of the plan included remodeling the original space. Camping gear is located on the second floor of this building, while offices and the warehouse occupy the other two floors.

Wide spaces were planned between the fixtures to accommodate traffic. All fixtures were custom-built of natural wood and are based on stocking needs determined by turnover of specific merchandise items.

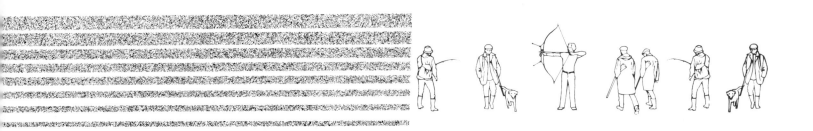

The challenge was to create a coherent design which would not draw attention to itself. All walls, ceilings, beams and posts were constructed by laminating layers of wood. Only two natural wood stains were used and signs were lettered with Bean's traditional green. The green was carried through in the carpeting in the men's area.

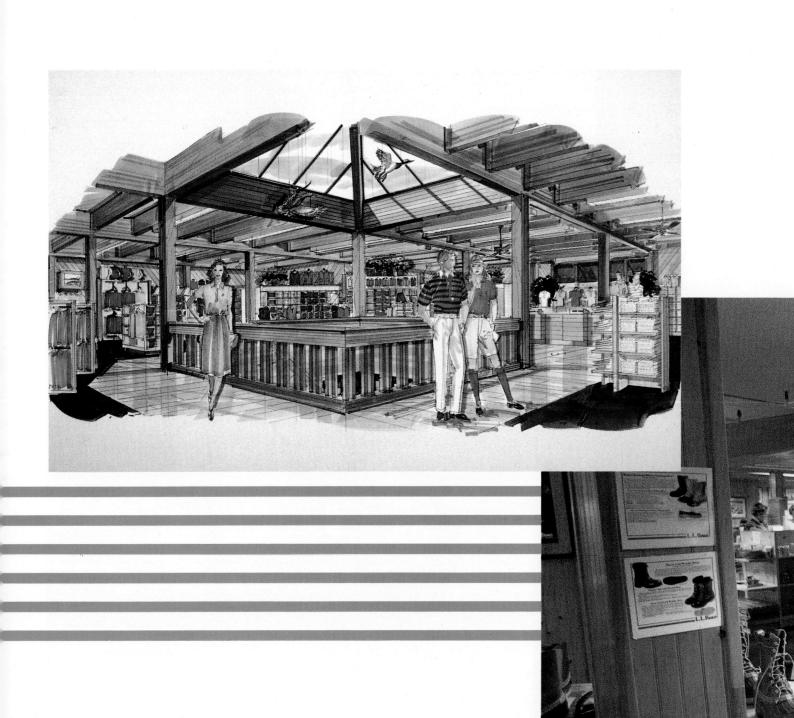

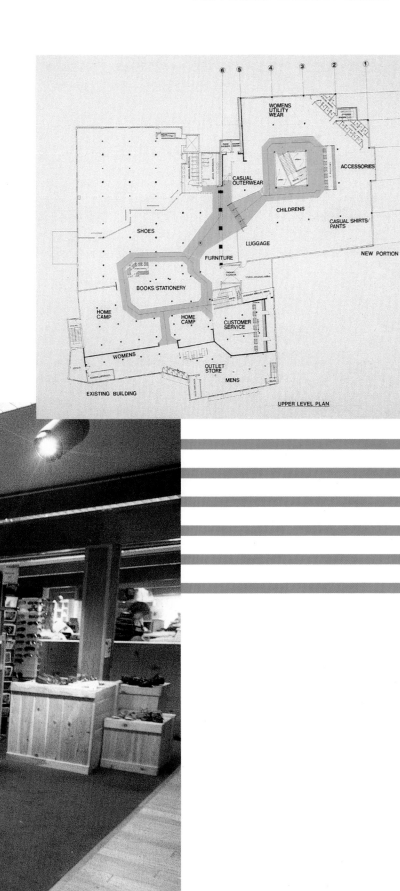

UPPER LEVEL PLAN

Parisian

Madison Square Mall
Huntsville, Alabama

Designed by: Schafer Associates
Oakbrook, Illinois

Honorable Mention, Soft Goods Specialty Stores

Parisian was created from the ground up to dominate the shopping mall in which it's located. The building exterior expresses the multi-level interior by means of a large glass wall, allowing a view of the store's central plaza from outside.

The central plaza, with its abundant natural light and ample seating, was designed as a place for people watching and as a stage for the store's special events. The decoration, both here and throughout the store, blends old and new elements almost effortlessly, expressing both the area's heritage and its commitment to the future.

Parisian departs from other contemporary designs along several fronts. First, the ceilings are of one height throughout for a greater uniformity. These ceilings are tinted in a single color, to minimize distractions and keep shoppers' eyes on the merchandise.

Also, the aisles are shorter than might be expected in this size of space, and they are shaped with a variety of angles along their length. This approach was used to encourage circulation and to provide more focal points for merchandise along the aisle.

Project: Parisian
Location: Madison Square Mall
Huntsville, Alabama
Client: Parisian

Both the exterior and the entranceway to Parisian were designed to dominate the shopping center and exert enough attraction to become the primary mall entrance.

INTERIOR DESIGN TEAM

Planner: Robert Schafer
Designers: Charles Sparks, Dale Wennlund
Decorator: Holly Lang
Job Captain: George Zachotina
Project Manager: John Salemi
Partner in charge: Robert Schafer
President: Robert Schafer
Consultants: Lighting By Design, APKC Architects
Contractors: Doster Construction, HBSA

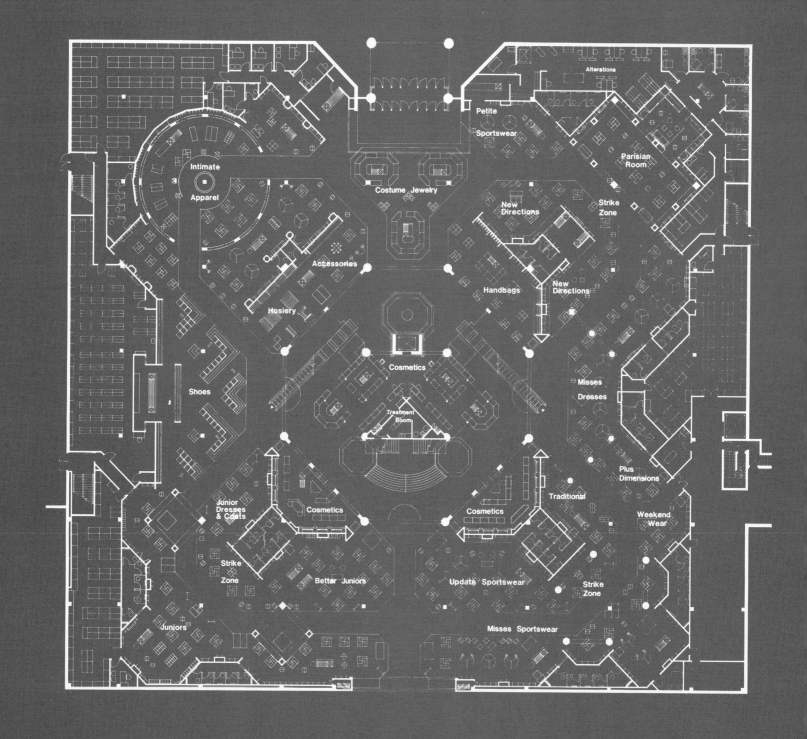

Intimate Apparel

Costume Jewelry

Petite Sportswear

Parisian Room

New Directions

Strike Zone

Accessories

Handbags

New Directions

Hosiery

Cosmetics

Misses Dresses

Shoes

Treatment Room

Plus Dimensions

Junior Dresses & Coats

Cosmetics

Cosmetics

Traditional

Weekend Wear

Strike Zone

Better Juniors

Update Sportswear

Strike Zone

Juniors

Misses Sportswear

Alterations

The entranceway is a multi-level open space called "Parisian Plaza." A skylight affords abundant natural light, and the area is used not only as a meeting place but as a stage for special store events. Escalators descend from the upper level to the side of the plaza away from the mall entrance, bringing customers past cosmetics, jewelry, and sportswear if returning to the mall, or past hosiery, accessories and costume jewelry if exiting to the parking lot.

The interior architecture reflects the sense of the community—a blend of the old and new. Touches such as pedestal fountains and gingerbread detailing recall the region's past, while the use of glass, tile, drop lights, and hanging fabric clearly identify it with the present.

The floor plan provides easy traffic flow throughout the store, bringing customers through and by all departments. Aisles are shaped to encourage circulation and to expose customers to a great variety of merchandise.

The tinted ceiling draws more attention to the merchandise and to the sightlines. Unlike many current designs, Parisian employs a ceiling of a single height to give an impression of uniformity. Still, the ambiance of specialty stores is preserved through the use of dividers and signage. Equal emphasis was placed on designing for both men and women, as Parisian's male customers do more of their own shopping than has been common in the past.

On the upper level, the use of complimentary materials provides easy visual integration to two very different areas, a David's Cookies counter with cafe-style seating and the bed/linens department.

The traffic plan provides easy flow throughout the store, exposing shoppers to all departments. The aisles are shaped into shorter segments to encourage easy circulation and provide more exposure along the aisles for merchandise. Best-of-class merchandise is located at critical circulation points, such as the entryways and bends in aisles.

HARD GOODS SPECIALTY STORES

ServiStar
Longview, Texas

Robert Floyd
Palm Desert, California

The key to design of the hard goods specialty stores is organization. The days of the cluttered hardware store and the clerk with the encyclopedic knowledge of it are gone forever. In these days of self-service, organization is everything.

Thus in the design of ServiStar, the purpose was to bring together all the individual elements of a particular job so that the customer can find whatever he or she needs, for example, in gardening, or rewiring a lamp.

The ServiStar prototype store designed by Retail Planning Associates goes one step further in its organizational planning. A central island displays the strictly hardware elements—hand and power tools, electrical and plumbing supplies, and similar items. Around the periphery is the non-hardware merchandise—housewares, lawn and garden supplies, etc. The loop running around the island provides full-circuit traffic around the entire store, exposing the customer to the entire range of merchandise.

Further organization is supplied by color-coding the merchandise in terms of quality. The ServiStar corporate colors of red and blue used on the merchandise are found throughout the store. In terms of easy "shopability," this concept is a superb example.

The problem of organization is solved in a different manner by Naomi Leff and Associates in their design of the Robert Floyd store in Palm Desert. Direction of the customer to a desired area is essential for a store with a wide diversity of merchandise ranging from fine china to plastic pool toys. This store with three axes within an overall circular design direct the customer to the specific category or object he or she is seeking.

The design concept of the hard goods specialty stores shown in this chapter utilizes a system of axes. The shopper chooses one axis which allows him to easily pass through the entire store. Merchandise is organized by category and arranged for easy self-service. Although each axis may have a distinct color, fixture, or type of product displayed, fixtures are uniform and are a unifying element to the store's overall design.

Without a large sales staff, the hard goods specialty store can still serve both its own needs and those of the customer through innovative design and organization.

ServiStar

Longview, Texas

Designed by: Retail Planning Associates, Inc.
Columbus, Ohio

Honorable Mention, Hard Goods Specialty Stores

Charged with creating a prototype store for the nationally-franchised ServiStar home centers, the designers incorporated a number of concepts new to the chain.

First, all hardware items such as hand and power tools, electrical and plumbing supplies, were located in the center of the store in a core island. Home center merchandise and housewares, such as paint, wall treatments, and lawn and garden supplies, were placed around the perimeter. Second, the four interior corners of the building were squared off to 45° angles, and the flat areas were used to display large graphics showing the store's products in use. Departments with heavy do-it-yourself appeal, such as paints, were located in these corners.

Besides these innovations, the designers had to use the ServiStar corporate colors, red and blue, for the store's interior. Red and blue are also used on packaging for ServiStar's private label goods. Standard quality products are packaged in black, good quality products in blue, and the best quality products in red and blue.

To enhance the contemporary look of the facility, no ceiling was installed, leaving the structural elements of the roof exposed. In addition, department signs were constructed of white neon in a script lettering and placed against a dark gray background accented with a polished chrome wire grid.

Project: ServiStar
Location: Longview, Texas
Client: American Hardware Supply Co.
           Butler, Pennsylvania

The challenge in designing this new 12,000-square-foot
prototype store for ServiStar, a nationally-franchised
hardware/home center chain, was to give it a contemporary style while retaining the corporation's existing signature colors, primarily red and blue.

INTERIOR DESIGN TEAM

Planner: Michael E. Murphy
Designers: Michael E. Murphy, H. Butch Belszek
Job Captain: Michael E. Murphy
Project Manager: Michael E. Murphy
V.P. in charge: William R. Sands
President: Michael J. Gade
Supplies: Childs Fixtures, Plastic Designs Inc. (neon)

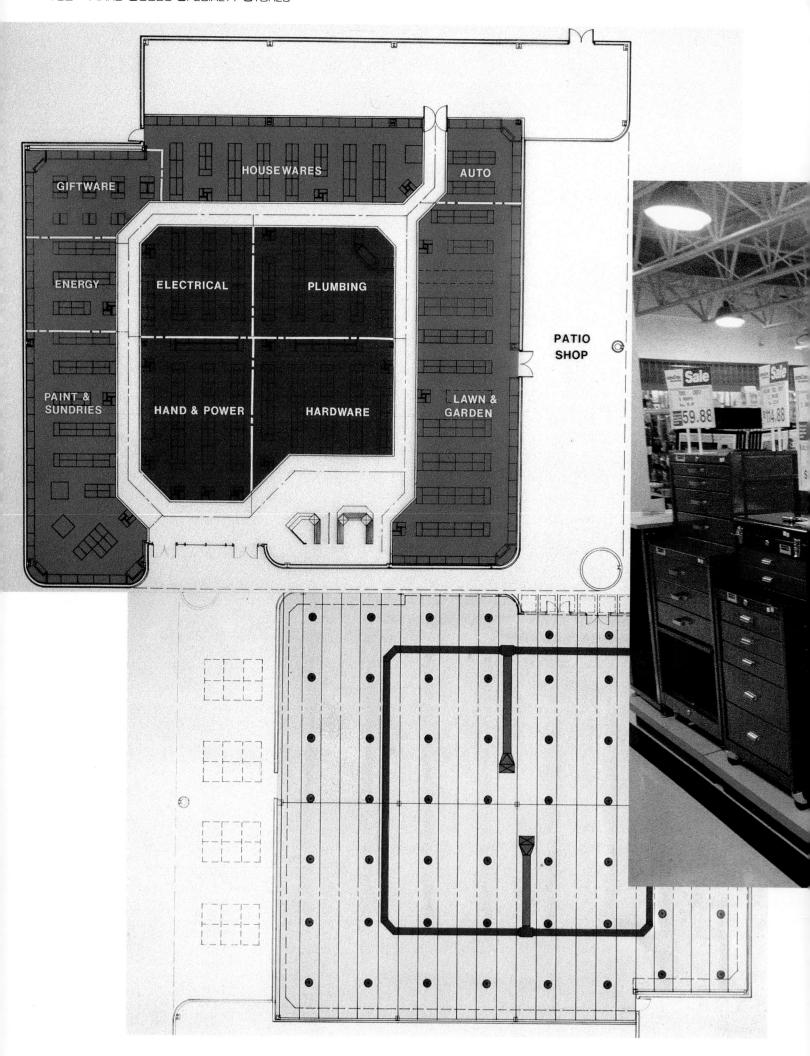

GIFTWARE

HOUSEWARES

AUTO

ENERGY

ELECTRICAL

PLUMBING

PATIO SHOP

PAINT & SUNDRIES

HAND & POWER

HARDWARE

LAWN & GARDEN

The layout features a loop to promote circulation through and by all merchandise displays. All hardware items—hand and power tools, electrical, and plumbing—were placed in the center island while non-hardware goods were located around the perimeter walls.

Standard fixtures were used throughout the store. In addition to carding merchandise on standard pegboards, quarter-inch diameter chrome wire grids were used on unique four-way fixtures. Fixture hardware, such as baskets and signage, can be attached to the grid.

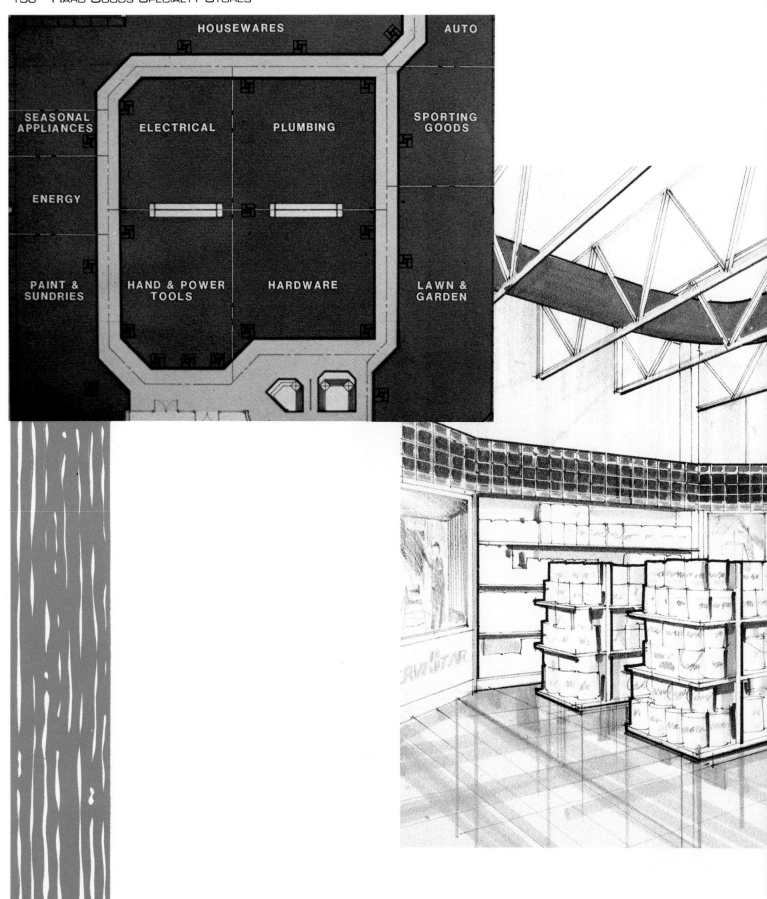

To help customers identify with do-it-yourself items, the building's four interior corners were given a 45° chamfer treatment. These angles were used to showcase three-foot-by-four-foot backlighted photographic transparencies showing the product in use.

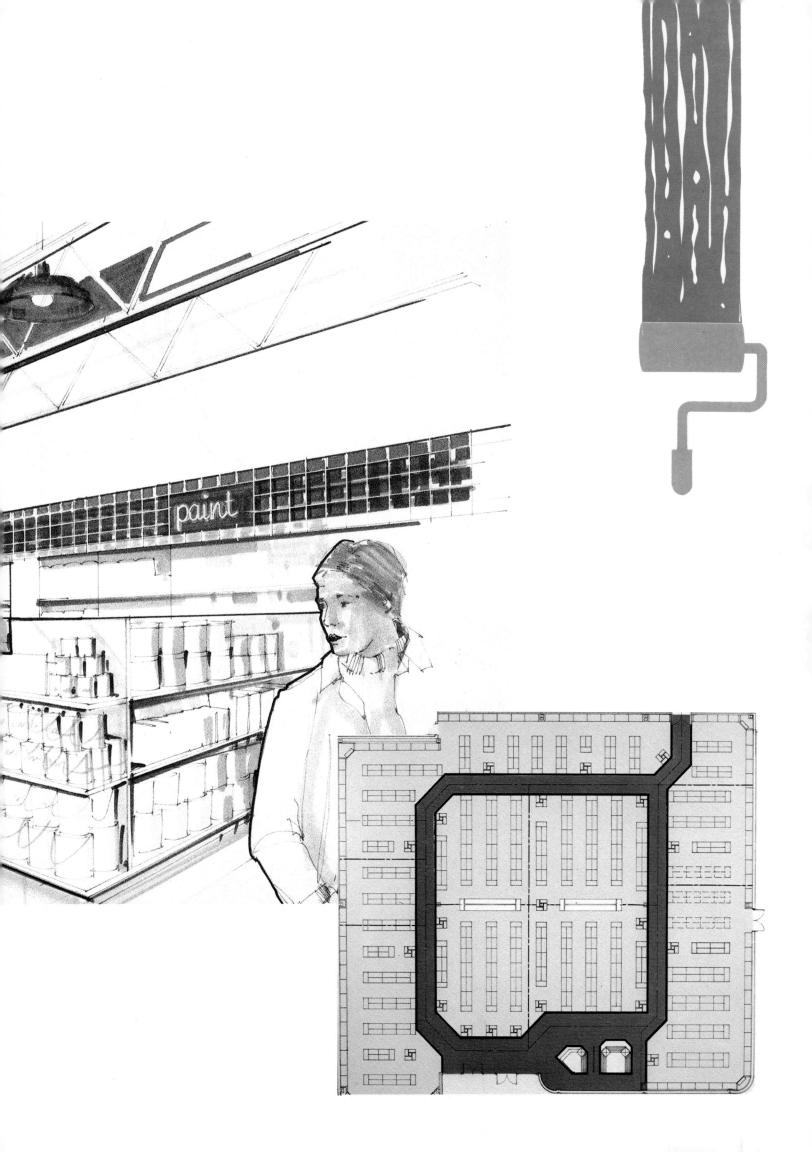

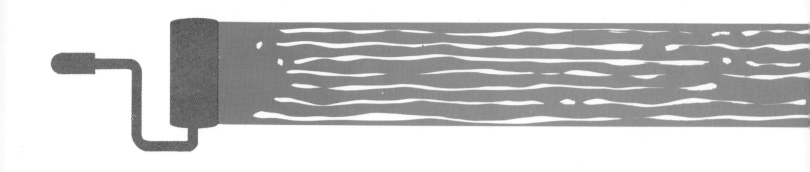

For departmental signage, white neon script lettering
was placed against a glossy, dark gray background and
accented with a six-inch square grid of polished chrome
wire.

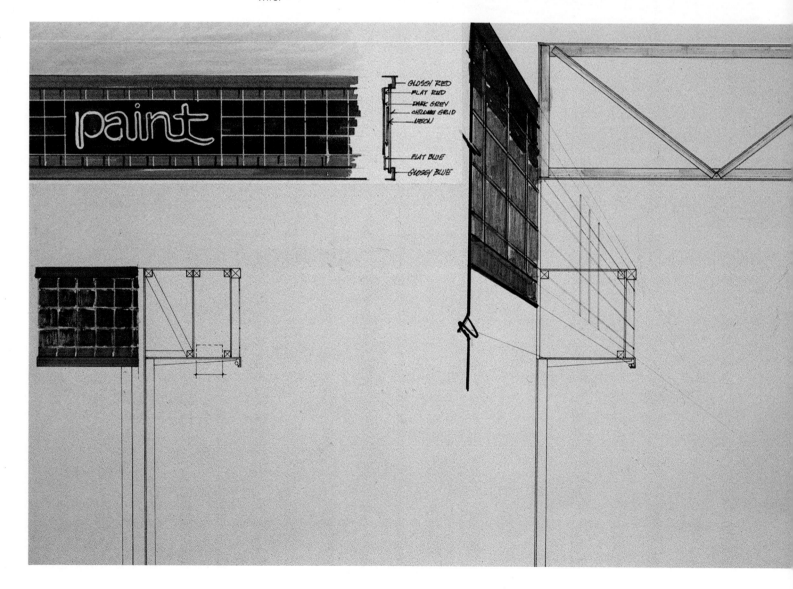

SERVISTAR

The wire grid four-way fixtures were primarily used for promotional features and were located in strategic selling locations. The fixture endcaps incorporate both "how to" display panels and informational pamphlets offering shopping checklists for common do-it-yourself projects.

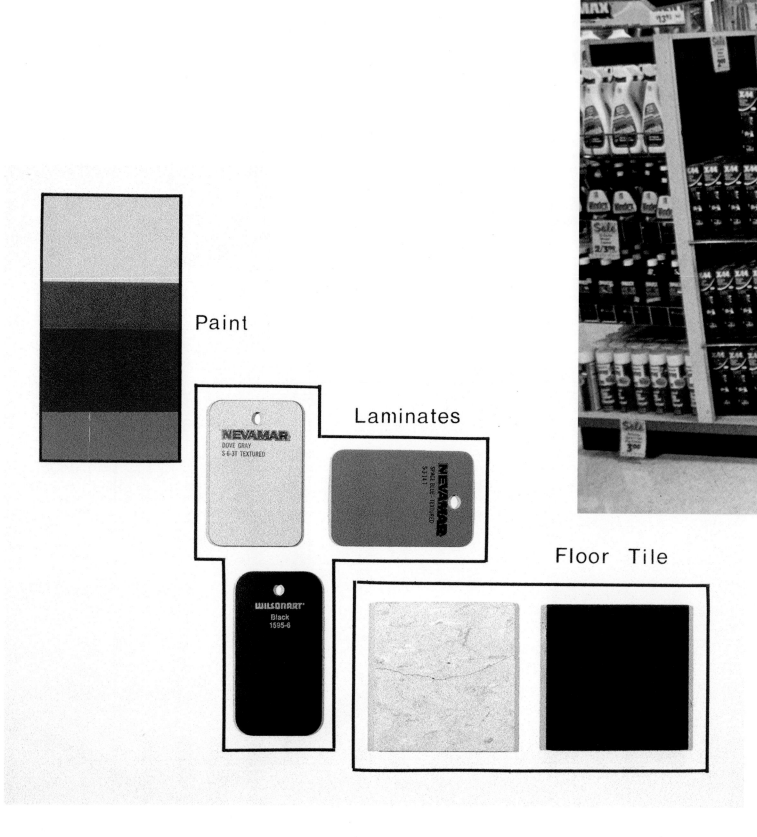

Paint

Laminates

Floor Tile

ServiStar's corporate colors were incorporated into a carefully planned graphics program. The chain uses colors in its packaging to indicate product quality. Standard products are packaged in black, better grades in blue, and the best quality in red and blue. This established heirarchy of colors was adopted as the theme for the prototype store.

Light gray vinyl tile flooring includes a black stripe to define aisles and promote circulation. The fixture bases were also darkened.

The illustrations used on the chamfers and point of sale materials were designed to complement the theme colors of the products. All signage was incorporated into the store itself—there are no hanging signs.

Fluorescent lights are used only under the perimeter cornices. The only other lighting consists of hanging 24-inch industrial fixtures fitted with high-intensity discharge bulbs.

The structural elements of the ceiling were left exposed to reinforce the upscale, high-tech feeling of the overall design. To minimize competition with the products and to keep customers' eyes on the displays, the ceiling was painted light gray.

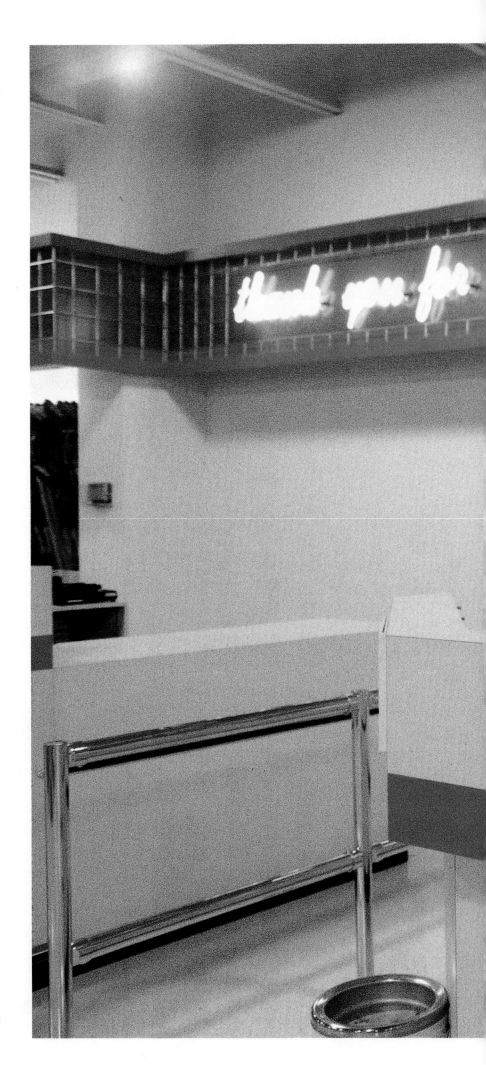

The treatment of departmental signs was repeated at
the information desk. Seen against the dark background,
the neon gleam enriches the upscale look of the facility.
A blue stripe was used as the dominant accent for the
perimeter cornice, helping to stop the shoppers' eye from
rising above the seven-foot high merchandise displays.

Robert Floyd

Palm Desert Town Center
Palm Desert, California

Designed by: Naomi Leff and Associates, Inc.
New York, New York

Honorable Mention, Hard Goods Specialty Stores

Though relatively small, 8,000 square feet, this Robert Floyd store had to accommodate a vast and disparate selection of items related to entertaining at home. The goods ranged from fine china and crystal to plastic kitchen utensils, presenting a diverse array of colors and textures.

Encouraging customers to walk through each display area was deemed critical. Three strong axes were layed out, separating the presentation areas for the different caliber goods: dinnerware to the right, a series of gift areas straight ahead, and housewares to the left. Shoppers have the option of choosing any one of the three areas to explore first, and cross aisles within the store allow traffic to flow smoothly among the departments.

A distinctive color palette was chosen for each axis. To tie the elements together and encourage recognition of the Robert Floyd name, the company's signature logo and corporate colors—red and black—were used as accents throughout.

The crystal and dinnerware displays are particularly effective. Black granite, black lacquer, gray carpets, gray velvet, red accents, and dramatic lighting showcase the elegant china. The display for crystal was done in dark gray suede, which absorbs light. This moderates the amount of light being reflected by the crystal from the walls and ceiling, and creates contrast, allowing highlights created by overhead spots to show clearly.

Project: Robert Floyd
Location: Palm Desert Town Center,
             Palm Desert, California
Client: Robert Floyd

This new 8,000-square-foot Robert Floyd had to be designed to showcase a wide range of household wares,
from elegant dinnerware and rare antiques to casual
kitchen utensils and plastic pool items.

INTERIOR DESIGN TEAM

Designer: Naomi Leff
Decorator: Jack Lowrance
Job Captain: Frank Nigro
Project Manager: Lawrence Adams
President: Naomi Leff
Consultants: Jack Lowrance (interior design),
                   Architectural Lighting Design (lighting)
Contractors: Hardesty Construction (general),
                   Amberg/Hinzman (cabinets)
                   Industrial Electric (lighting)
Supplies: Stark Carpets, Inc., Maharam Fabric Co.,
                   Lightolier

In the opulent Dinnerware Gallery, a dark, dramatic scheme was chosen to show off the merchandise. Black granite, black lacquer, gray carpet, gray velvets, red accents, and lighting combine to focus attention on dinnerware, linens, and Lalique crystal.

The marketing concept depends on customers circulating throughout the store. Three strong traffic axes were created, and after passing through the black-and-red themed entrance, customers must choose one of these three pathways. The Dinnerware Gallery is to the right, a series of Gift Galleries terminating in a semi-circular area for antiques is straight ahead, and housewares are to the left.

Although each axis has a distinct pattern of materials, finish, and colors, the design is unified through the repetition of black, gray, and red, and the use of lacquered archways between departments. Here, a simulated skylight enhances the presentation of silk flowers.

The Crystal Gallery was executed entirely in soft grays.
The gray absorbs light, increasing the visual contrast and
allowing the crystal to sparkle with highlights from the
overhead spot fixtures.

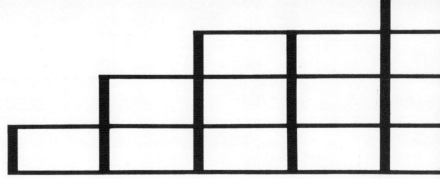

The housewares section is the least formal area, with the casual styling and materials chosen to provide a suitable display of plastics and assorted kitchen implements. The signature black and red are used as a unifying theme.

DEPARTMENT STORE
FLOOR RENOVATIONS

Younkers
Des Moines, Iowa

Rich's
Atlanta, Georgia

I. Magnin
San Francisco, California

With the floor renovation, the designer is faced with a similar situation as the renovation of an entire store, only on a smaller scale. The fact is that a single floor need not have any design similarities with other floors (except, perhaps, for weight bearing walls, plumbing, and similar structural "constants"). Thus the renovated floor can stand by itself as a single example of redesign.

As has been mentioned earlier, one of the leading trends in department stores across the country is the elimination of the large sales staff in favor of a few strategically placed cashiers. As the customer is left more and more on his or her own, the need for the open sightlines and easily definable departments becomes more and more evident. "Easy to shop" and "shopability" become passwords in the field.

Thus in redesigning the Younkers in Des Moines, Schaefer Associates stressed the need for an open plan with few walls and open sightlines. Straight aisles, with ceiling design reinforcing the circulation pattern, makes the store easy to shop by providing the customer with the help and direction he or she wants. The success of the renovation is apparent in more than design terms—sales increased by 300 percent over earlier store sales.

The floor renovation done by CNI International for Rich's department store in Atlanta was directed toward appealing to a more sophisticated market. In the children's department, the designers introduced contemporary design elements, moving away from the theme orientation and toward a look that was less and less obviously one of a children's department. The other department on the floor, the electronics section, lent itself more easily to renovation, and here the designers went all out for state of the art decor. A dark green color scheme gives a strong all-encompassing feeling that lets the customer feel as if he or she were in a completely closed and private world. Thus within a single floor the goals of upscaling and improving "shopability" are satisfied and set the tone for future changes in the rest of the store.

Younkers

Des Moines, Iowa

Designed by: Schafer Associates
Oak Brook, Illinois

First Award, Department Store Floor Renovations

In remodeling the street level of the main Younkers location, the designers were asked to realign circulation patterns to allow shoppers to move from the men's area to women's and back easily. Also, the store is located in Des Moines' main business district. So the design had to reduce the time pressure on busy office workers, perhaps shopping on their lunch break.

The original selling floor was divided by a number of physical barriers, such as elevators, stairwells, mechanical shafts, and a service alley. These were removed or repositioned to create a contiguous selling floor. In the women's area, the center of the floor was left open, with departments delineated by glass dividers.

This allows an unobstructed view of the cosmetics and accessories departments. The men's area, however, was divided into a number of specialty shops, each with its own "storefront" and displays.

Visually, the new floor was modeled on the previously renovated lower floor, called The Metropolis. "New Directions" merchandise is highlighted in special displays and an area was added for men's cosmetics to demonstrate the store's responsiveness to younger shoppers.

Project: Younkers
Location: Des Moines, Iowa
Client: Younkers

In renovating the street floor of Younkers main store, the designers were asked to style the space after the store's adventurous lower level called The Metropolis.

INTERIOR DESIGN TEAM

Planner:	R.H. Lubben
Designer:	Charles Sparks
Decorator:	Holly Lang
Job Captain:	Bruce Hamilton
Project Manager:	Mark Johnson
V.P. in charge:	R.H. Lubben
Consultant:	Estelle Ellison
Contractors:	J.R. Jones Fixtures, Goebel Fixtures, Carlson Fixtures, Neuman Construction Co., Baker Electric

During the renovation, elevators, stairwells, mechanical shafts, partitions, and other physical barriers were relocated to create a contiguous selling floor. This, it was felt, would ease movement from men's to women's selling areas and emphasize that Younkers is for both men and women.

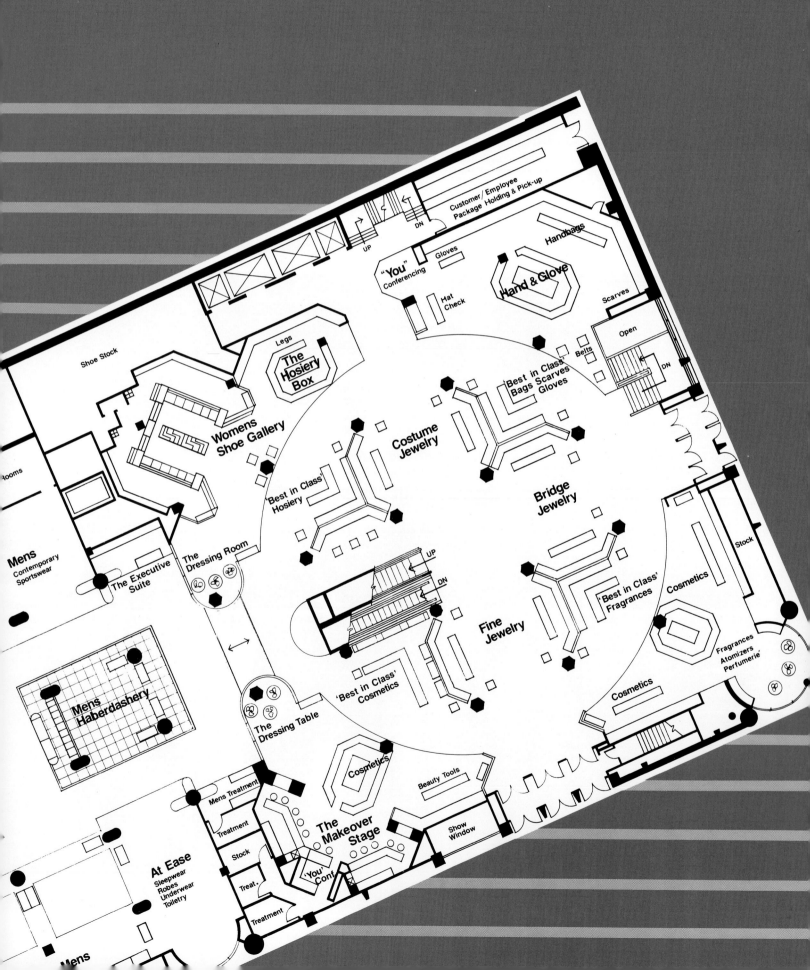

Customer / Employee Package Holding & Pick-up

"You" Conferencing

Gloves

Handbags

Hand & Glove

Hat Check

Scarves

Open

Belts

Best in Class Bags Scarves Gloves

Legs

The Hosiery Box

Shoe Stock

Womens Shoe Gallery

Costume Jewelry

Bridge Jewelry

'Best in Class' Hosiery

Stock

Rooms

Mens Contemporary Sportswear

The Executive Suite

The Dressing Room

Best in Class' Fragrances

Cosmetics

Fine Jewelry

'Best in Class' Cosmetics

Cosmetics

Fragrances Atomizers Perfumerie

Mens Haberdashery

The Dressing Table

Cosmetics

Beauty Tools

Mens Treatment

Treatment

The Makeover Stage

Show Window

At Ease
Sleepwear
Robes
Underwear
Toiletry

Stock

Treat.

'You' Conf

Treatment

Mens

In the cosmetics section, as in other areas, best-in-class merchandise is highlighted by special display treatment opposite the general merchandise offerings.

In both men's and women's areas, signature features, architecture, and colors were used to identify the various customer segments.

The men's area, unlike the open-plan women's area, uses a storefront approach, creating a street of specialty shops offering more or less formal clothing. Contemporary clothing is showcased to demonstrate the store's responsiveness to younger buyers, and a men's treatment area was added to handle male cosmetics.

An octagonal floor plan was used in the women's area, creating unobstructed sightlines across the main selling floor. Glazed dividers and carefully engineered lighting open up the store visually.

Rich's

Cumberland Mall
Atlanta, Georgia

Designed by: CNI International
New York, New York

Honorable Mention, Department Store Floor Renovations

The new first floor for Rich's in Atlanta's Cumberland Mall divides the selling floor into three distinct zones, a men's world, children's world, and an electronics area called Sights & Sounds. A strong aisle system was developed to encourage circulation and to allow shoppers to grasp the layout at a glance. Variations in ceiling height were used to define both the aisle and the various departments.

The three zones are distinctly different in coloration, texture, and design. The palette used in the men's area is subtle and ranges from black lacquer, through charcoal, walnut, bronze, and sepia to beige. Children's World, in the center of

the store, is floored with brick-pattern teak blocks. Brightly-colored lacquer panels complement the vivid merchandise. Pyramidal gazebos were placed beneath trompe l'oeil skys in three plazas at the intersection of major aisles. Stainless steel, neon, and a deep green carpet set a high-tech tone for Sights & Sounds. A continuous neon strip pulls shoppers into the area's inner core and defines individual departments. The effect is one of a sleek and highly-focused selling environment.

Project: Rich's (lower mall level)
Location: Cumberland Mall
Atlanta, Georgia
Client: Rich's
Design Firm: CNI International
New York, New York

Children's World is defined by brick-patterned teak-block flooring and many lacquered and contrasting planes of color. A trompe l'oeil skylight appears on the ceiling.

INTERIOR DESIGN TEAM

Planner:	Frank Sluzas
Designer:	Tom Tarnowski
Decorator:	Patty Madden
Project Manager:	Gerald Brienza
Partner in charge:	Robert Herbert
President/Chairman:	Lawrence Israel
Consultants:	Stevens & Wilkinson
Contractors:	M.E.I. (Merchandising Equipment)
	H.B.S.A. (Hochberg Bros.)
Suppliers:	Perma-Grain - wood flooring
	Robbins - wood flooring

Sights & Sound makes its strong and highly
contemporary design statement with stainless steel
columns framing the entrance and neon strips drawing
the customer in toward the central counter.

The continuous neon strip around the perimeter defines
every department. Scored, brushed stainless steel panels
recall the entry columns, separating areas and creating a
sleek and highly focused selling environment.

Herringbone-patterned aisles of walnut-stained oak lead the customer through the departments of Men's World.

The overall plan involved the creation of a zonal plan with a series of contemporary worlds—Men's World, Children's World, and Sights & Sounds. Traffic is defined by a cross-axial grid, and all aisles are major ones.

Strong architectural elements such as columns and wood paneling enhance the contemporary look of individual departments. Bright woods, glass partitioning, and beige lacquer-cube grid ceilings define a designer sportswear area with a crisp, clean appearance.

I. Magnin

Union Square
San Francisco, California

Designed by: Walker/Group, Inc.
New York, New York

Honorable Mention, Department Store Floor Renovations

The work done on the main I. Magnin store, in San Francisco, was both renovation and a return to the past. The historic facility has been part of the city's Union Square shopping district for more than half a century. Over the years, a variety of "improvements" gradually masked much of the original, opulent design.

During the remodeling, the magnificent two-story central bay was restored to its original condition. The bay's Lalique light fixtures were reconditioned, and some new functional elements were added to the original 1930's showcases to make them more useful.

The mezzanine was converted to a series of fine shops with simple glass facades, and an overlook was built into the escalator landing to allow shoppers a view of the central selling floor below.

The basement storage area was converted into sales space. Men's World takes in 11,000 square feet, and Edibles, a food store, takes in 5,000 square feet. The basement, ground floor, mezzanine, and seventh floors were created by the designers, and the intermediate floors were designed by I. Magnin's own store planners.

Project:	I. Magnin
Location:	Union Square, San Francisco, California
Client:	Federated Department Stores Cincinnati, Ohio

The I. Magnin store in San Francisco's Union Square is very much a part of the city's heritage. Unlike neighboring stores, Saks, Neiman-Marcus, and Macy's, Magnin's management chose to renovate the graceful older building and restore much of it to the original design.

INTERIOR DESIGN TEAM

Designer:	Masako Endo
Planners:	Eric Jacobs, Paula Caravelli, Lauren Yost
Decorator:	Ed Sierra
Job Captain:	Evangelo Dascal
Project Manager:	Arturo Melero
V.P. in charge:	Raul Nunez
President:	Kenneth H. Walker
Consultants:	T. Sehulster Architects
Contractors:	Plant Builders, Inc., Unger Fuss Co.
Supplies:	Marble Supply International, Inc. Messmore & Damon, Inc.

One key to the plan was the installation of an escalator
bank in the corner of the store adjacent to Union
Square. The escalators lead up to a mezzanine which
was replanned as a series of shops with simple, glazed
facades.

Stationary

Hermes

Luggage

Fendi

First Floor below

Ferragamo

Chanel

Botega Veneta

Beauty Salon

An overlook carved out of the escalator bank gives customers a dramatic view of the first floor of this retailing landmark. The basement, ground floor, mezzanine, and seventh floor were executed by the designers, while Magnin's in-house staff handled the renovation of the intermediate floors.

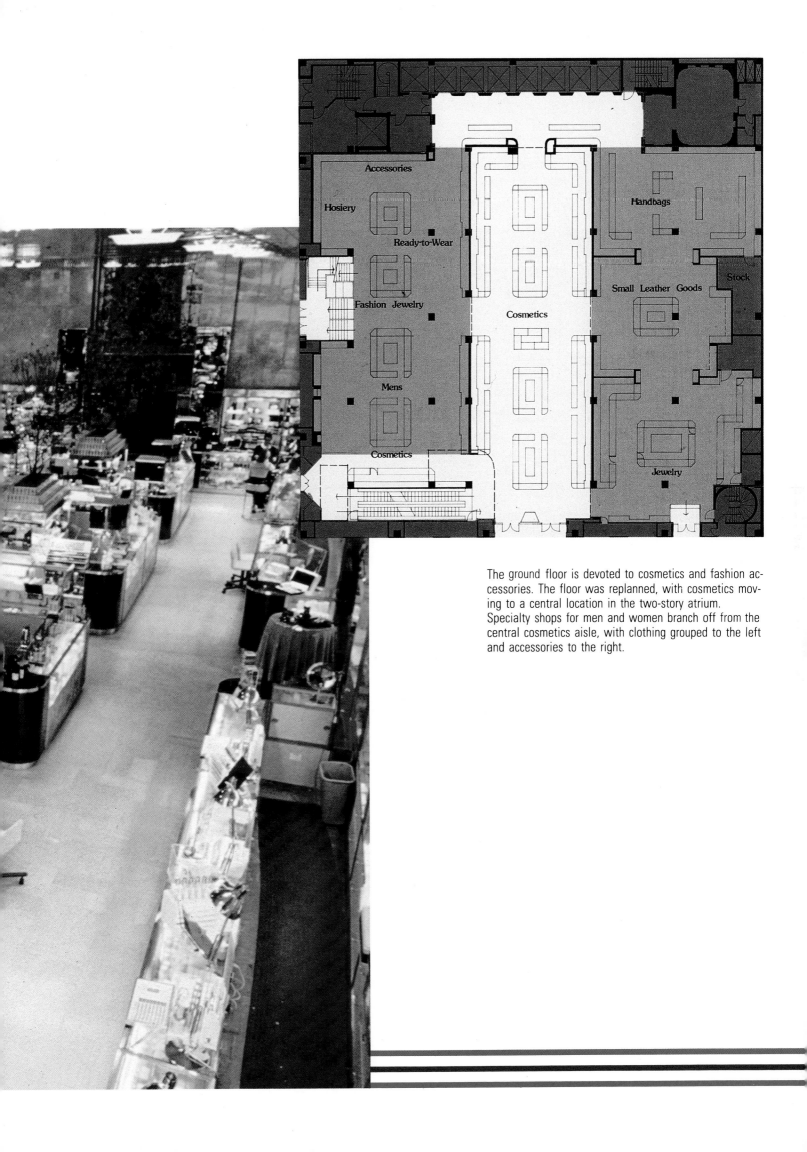

The ground floor is devoted to cosmetics and fashion accessories. The floor was replanned, with cosmetics moving to a central location in the two-story atrium.
Specialty shops for men and women branch off from the central cosmetics aisle, with clothing grouped to the left and accessories to the right.

The two-story atrium, with its Lalique light fixtures and pink marble walls, was also restored to its original specifications.

The original showcases, manufactured in the 1930's, were restored and blended with more contemporary elements to make them more functional.

General
Merchandise Stores

Perry Ellis Shoes
New York, New York

Collar Bar
Las Vegas, Nevada

Nathan Alan Fine Jewelry
Costa Mesa, California

The planning of a small store specializing in a particular type or even a line of clothing is an interesting challenge to the store designer. For one thing, the space with which he is given to work may be extremely small. Within this space, the designer must provide space for special display, for trying on, and for general presentation of merchandise, as well as storage and office space. Many of the needs of the larger store—sightlines, aisle space, departmental differentiation—are not considerations here. In terms of merchandise, instead of profusion, the key word in the smaller store is selection, and the designer must be aware at all times of this difference.

The word most frequently used to describe the Perry Ellis shoe store designed by Hambrecht Terrell is "jewel box." This is, indeed, an exquisite little store. Only 600 square feet in size, the shop is a showplace for the display and sale of the designer's footwear. Several different light grids are used, so that at night in particular, when the shop is closed, shoes or groupings of shoes can be easily displayed to the passerby.

The materials used in this shop, which is a prototype for future Perry Ellis shoe shops, are the same as those in the firm's corporate offices, which were also designed by Hambrecht Terrell. Polished English sycamore, marble, mirrors, leather, and gray glass predominate. A horizontal 18-inch band which appears on the glassed-in offices of the corporate headquarters, appears on the mirrored walls of the store. Thoroughly contemporary, the look is also elegant, European, and exquisite.

The ability of the small store to make a specific fashion statement has been carefully noted by the Planned Expansion Group in designing the Collar Bar in Las Vegas. Specializing in shirts and men's accessories, the store is designed to get every inch of display and coordination into its small quarters. Yet, despite all this, the feeling is calm, open, uncluttered. The ability to lodge a strong statement into a small space is typical of the best in small clothing store design today.

The location of a store can also dictate a fashion statement. Take, for example, Nathan Alan Fine Jewelry in Costa Mesa, California's, trendy South Coast Plaza. This store, formerly Riches Jewelry, was redesigned, renovated, and enlarged. A new store front was created incorporating more show windows which doubled merchandise presentation. A second entrance was added improving circulation to and from its trend-setting area of the mall. But, by far, the most unique feature in this store is its staff, who dressed in black tuxedos, greet customers with a glass of champagne.

Each of the stores in this chapter, although unique in their merchandise and design, have a unifying goal. That is to combine efficient, orderly, yet lively display of their merchandise in the space available. Merchandise display is limited by the size of the store, but good design can work around that.

Perry Ellis Shoes

New York, New York

Designed by: Hambrecht Terrell International
New York, New York

First Award, General Merchandise Stores

A fashion designer seeks to keep a fresh, updated image in front of the public constantly. The image must be conveyed within a consistent overall design philosophy which supports and reinforces the designer's own approach to design.

This store was created as a prototype, but had to reflect the design themes and materials used in existing Perry Ellis retail facilities. The existing locations are decorated with English sycamore, gray glass, and marble. The consistency underscores Ellis' identity, making it instantly recognizeable and helping to support each season's new merchandise.

In keeping with its location in New York's busy—and expensive—Madison Avenue shopping district, the store is only 600 square feet, and is much deeper than it is broad. Merchandise displays are kept fresh by using the lighting system, which includes individually-controlled pin spots, to selectively highlight different merchandise and groupings each night.

Project: Perry Ellis Shoes
Location: New York, New York
Client: Michael G. Abrams, Inc.
Design Firm: Hambrecht Terrell International
New York, New York

This small, 600-square-foot shop on New York's Madison Avenue was designed as a prototype for future Perry Ellis shoe shops. The styling is an extension of the Perry Ellis image, created in 1980 by architects who created the designer's original showroom.

INTERIOR DESIGN TEAM

Planner:	James. E. Terrell
Designers:	James E. Terrell, Michael J. McGowan
Job Captain:	Emilio Wong
Project Manager:	Michael J. McGowan
V.P. in charge:	Harve Oeslander
President/Chairman:	James E. Terrell, Edward C. Hambrecht
Consultant:	David A. Mintz (lighting)
Contractors:	Anton Waldman & Associates
	Syska & Hennessey (engineering)

A comfortable and elegant ambiance is achieved by the use of overstuffed furnishings and rich materials. Despite the small size, the store has a very open feeling.

The small size and deep, rectangular format reflect the surroundings. Shallow, wide retail spaces such as those common to suburban malls are seldom available in the heart of New York's Manhattan shopping district.

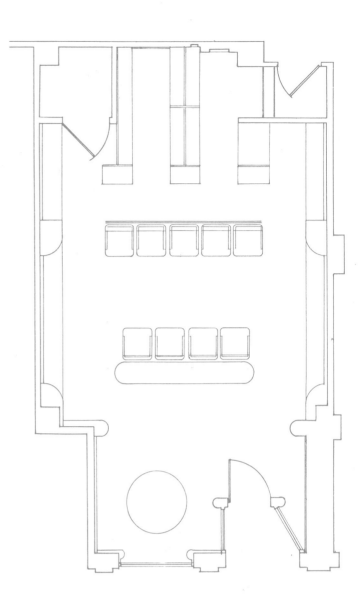

Slabs of gray glass separate the stock room from the sales area, yet keep it open to the floor and to the mirrors so that customers can easily see themselves wearing the shoes.

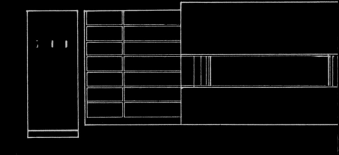

Broad recessed displays on opposite walls feature three lighting systems: a wall wash, general illumination, and low voltage accent lights to increase the drama of merchandise displayed there.

An unusual lighting system featuring low voltage pin spots controlled individually can be used to highlight individual shoes at night. The constantly changing visual statement appeals to the window shoppers and keeps interior from becoming a static image.

Collar Bar

Boulevard Mall
Las Vegas, Nevada

Designed by: Planned Expansion Group, Inc.
White Plains, New York

Honorable Mention, General Merchandise Stores

At less than 1,500 square feet, the Collar Bar was intended to serve as the prototype for a chain of small shops carrying only shirts, sweaters, belts, ties, and accessories.

A strong image was created for Collar Bar through the use of unique fixtures, precise layout, and colors. Two shades of gray were used throughout, and red appears as an accent.

The fixtures are custom designed for maximum flexibility. The freestanding displays can be converted to display folded shirts or hanging shirts quickly. The signature fixtures—the checkout, the belt display, and feature displays—work with the vaulted ceiling to reinforce Collar Bar's design identity. Although the range of fixtures is limited in the interest of consistency, fixture types alternate along both walls to sustain visual interest.

This consistency conveys a sense of order while the use of accent colors and contemporary shapes enlivens the store.

		INTERIOR DESIGN TEAM	
Project:	Collar Bar		
Location:	Boulevard Mall	Designer:	Robert W. Grzywacz
	Las Vegas, Nevada	Job captain:	Robert Rosit
Client:	Collar Bar, a division of	Partner in charge:	Matthew F. Kroin
	Edison Brothers Stores, Inc.,	Project manager:	Albert J. Krull
	St. Louis, Missouri	Consultants:	East House Enterprises (graphics)
Design Firm:	Planned Expansion Group,	Contractors:	Atmor Fixture and Construction Corp.
	White Plains, New York		

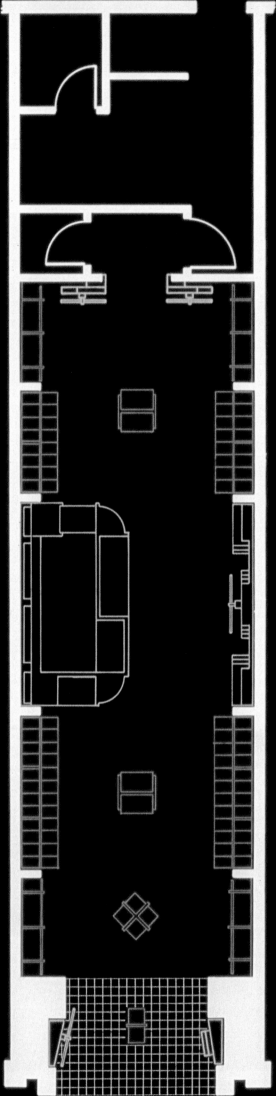

The Collar Bar is a chain of small stores, each under 1,500 square feet, which carries only shirts, ties, sweaters, belts, and accessories. Consistency is the key in making a strong design statement. This is seen both in the architectural elements, which use modular dimensions to provide a precise relationship among all the store's fixtures, and in color, which consists of two shades of gray for a neutral backdrop combined with red for accent. Everything is designed; there are no random elements.

A mirror at the back of the store gives an illusion
of greater depth. Visual interest is increased by
the use of actual merchandise as one of the design
elements, adding to the color scheme while at the same
time maintaining the architectural unity of the overall
design.

Despite the large number of items displayed in the store,
the design and fixtures combine to convey an orderly yet
lively and colorful presence that highlights, rather than
detracts from the merchandise.

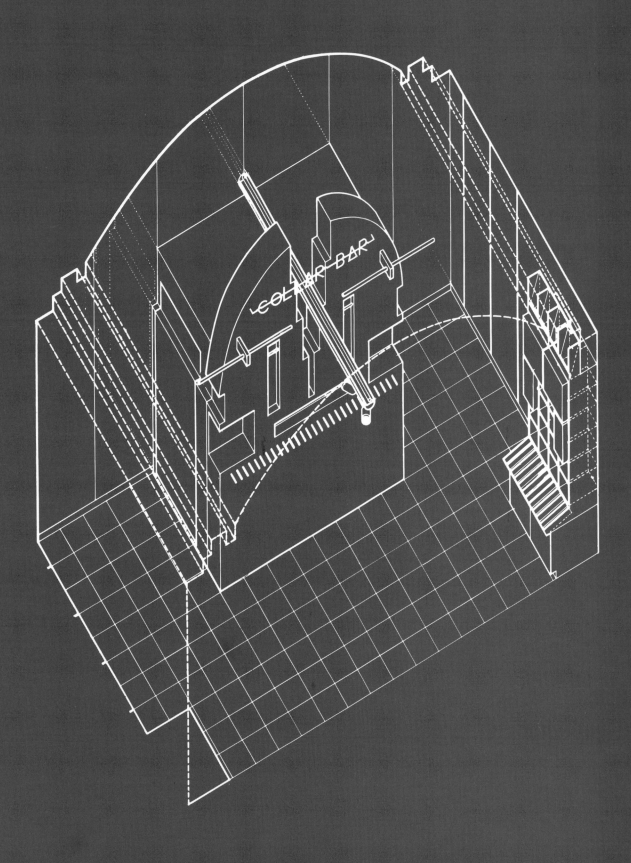

COLLAR-BAR

"Picture frames" for feature display of coordinated shirts and ties are designed to replace either two or four shirt bins. In addition to providing a display surface, they serve to conceal either back stock or understocked bins.

Freestanding display units are flexible, designed for simple conversion to accommodate either folded shirts in bins or hanging shirts on rods. Fixture types alternate along both walls to sustain visual interest. The clear, rather rigid designs of the display fixtures are balanced by the contrasting sculptural quality of the vaulted ceiling and signature fixtures.

Nathan Alan Fine Jewelry

South Coast Plaza
Costa Mesa, California

Designed by: The Bannister Group
Pasadena, California

Honorable Mention, General Merchandise Stores

The challenge in this project was to convert an existing jewelry store, Riches, into a high-line, service-oriented facility. The original store had 53 linear feet of mall frontage, but was only ten feet deep and had only one entrance.

The redesign added another 20 feet of frontage and 200 square feet. This created the space for another entrance and for a sit-down showcase seating eight and a repair service counter.

The store is located in an area of the mall with other stores that are considered leaders in their category. To appear consistent with this ambiance, the store's front, decoration, and fixtures were

overhauled. The entrances were framed in mahogany columns. The windows along the front were back-painted a crisp blue, and small feature display windows were created within them. The walls were faced with panels wrapped in blue-gray silk, and cove lighting was installed to provide a gentle, overall illumination. Pin spots highlight individual displays.

The store follows through on the promise of such an elegant design. The store staff dresses in tuxedoes, and as customers enter, each is given a glass of champagne.

Project: Nathan Alan Fine Jewelry
Location: South Coast Plaza,
Costa Mesa, California
Client: Alan Lemmerman

Nathan Alan Fine Jewelry was created from an existing jewelry store called Riches. The square footage was increased to include a sit-down showcase sales area and a new storefront constructed to accommodate display windows.

INTERIOR DESIGN TEAM

Planner: Mary Broerman
Designer: Christina-Scalise Adams
Decorator: Kristy Wilson
President: Stevie Bannister
Consultant: Francis Krahe & Associates (lighting)
Contractor: G.C.-R.C. Brown & Associates
Supplies: Wilson Showcase (showcase), Harbinger (carpet), S. Harris (wallcovering), Halo, Edison & Price (lighting), Barret Hill & Lowenstein (furniture)

The original store had 52 linear feet of mall frontage, yet was just ten feet deep and had only one entrance. The redesign incorporated 200 additional square feet in an adjacent space, allowing room for four sit-down cases with seating for eight customers.

20'-2" PROPOSED ADDITION   32'-4" EXISTING STORE

EXISTING PLANTER

SCALE: 3/8":1'-0"

N

The new storefront, constructed of glass, back-painted a
crisp blue, incorporates 16 show windows. Two dramatic, wood-framed entrances were created, emphasizing
the store's new identity and improving circulation patterns. A jewelry repair center was located so as to be
visible through the entrance, enticing customers and un-
derlining the store's commitment to personalized service.

The mahogany ceiling echoes the columns at the entrances and conceals the perimeter cove lighting which provides a soft general illumination. Low-voltage track lights highlight merchandise in the showcases. Black carpeting and black-trim, glass showcases were used to avoid pulling the customer's eye away from the merchandise. The harshness of the black is softened by the use of chairs upholstered in gray suede and wall panels wrapped in a soft, blue-gray silk.

SMALL STORES

Hair Sensations, the winner in this category, is the result of an eight to ten month study of the functions of a hairdressing salon. The result was a complete change in the traffic flow and a salon that appeals to a broad spectrum of clients.

The study conducted by RTR Designs, Inc. concluded that the patron had to walk too far and retrace her steps too frequently in the average salon. At Hair Sensations, the sink area is not all the way at the back of the salon but at the center, since the sinks, as RTR's Robert Roever notes, are the real heart of the salon, from permanents and coloring to a simple wash and blow-dry, involves the use of the sink.

With the sinks central to the plan, the traffic pattern of the entire establishment has been worked out so that the client need not move more than five feet in any direction to partake of any service. The traffic pattern is strongly reinforced by the custom-designed, low voltage lighting treatment, which is designed to hit the path between one function of the salon and the next.

Aside from layout, the designers decided to get away from what has become banal in the vocabulary of beauty salon decor. Moving away from the "crystalline" look of polished metal, mirrors, and ceramic tile, RTR chose to use a tropical palette of pastel blue, maize, and gray to complement the store's Miami location. In general, they sought to make Hair Sensations a salon that would appeal to a broader spectrum of clientele than the rather posh North Miami setting would initially seem to offer. To attract clients of all ages, they aimed for a "fun" type of environment—something that would provide the client with more entertainment than the usual ministrations of a beauty salon would provide. Thus, for example, the designers have thoughtfully placed a skylight over the sink area so that the client has something besides ceiling to look at while she sits with her head tilted back over the sink. All in all, this is a "user-friendly" environment designed to attract a variety of potential clients and keep them coming back.

Hair Sensations

Aventura Mall
Miami, Florida

Designed by: RTR Designs, Inc.
New York, New York

First Award, Small Stores

The traditional notions of defined traffic patterns aren't often applied to hair salons. As a result, they sometimes lack a defined circulation, and suffer from a loss of visual clarity.

In the 1,250-square-foot Hair Sensations, this problem was addressed without compromising the space devoted to the salon's functions.

A spectacular columned facade, reinforced with neon, faces out into the mall. A small reception area is centered in this entrance, welcoming the patrons, yet blocking a view of the shop interior. Shelves behind this reception area are used to stock and display salon hair products for retail sale.

Privacy was provided for the service cubicles by enclosing them with low retaining walls. The walls were topped by pipe railing and inset with square glass blocks. The railings rise into alternating arches and pediments. These classical elements were repeated across the aisle over the styling stations. The rhythm of this repetition ties the two areas together, yet the elements are executed in different materials, providing variety and visual interest.

Project: Hair Sensations
Location: Aventura Mall,
Miami, Florida
Client: Giorgio Castriota
Design Firm: RTR Designs, Inc.
New York, New York

INTERIOR DESIGN TEAM

Designers: Robert T. Roever, Clark D. Ruiz II
V.P. in charge: Robert T. Roever
Consultant: Steven Mendelsohn
Contractor: Raphael Construction
Supplies: Majestic Woodcrafts,
Wally Turner Custom Woodworking

Beyond the facade of this hair salon is a lighted reception desk and retail wall. With three other salons already open in this new mall, the challenge was to differentiate Hair Sensations through design without losing the functionality of a traditional salon layout.

Opulence was the intent of the facade, which opens into the mall's common space. The neon-reinforced columns house the tubing of the rolling grille used to secure the store after hours and supports a neon-reinforced archway.

Circulation through the salon is defined by two paths which flank the reception desk. A raised ceiling with a custom light fixture and the geometric pattern of the floor tiles outline these paths.

Service cubicles lie on one side of the salon's center line. The cubicles are entered through portals constructed of pipe railings. Square glass blocks set within a square opaque structure enhance the visual significance of the cubicles.

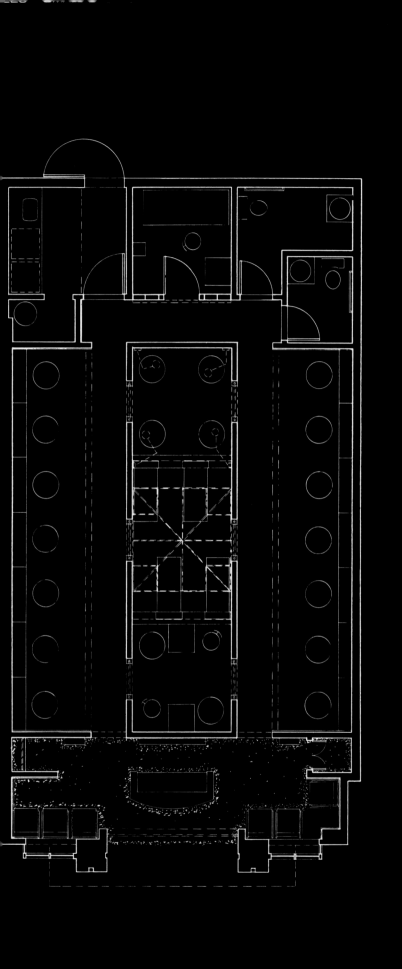

The visual rhythm set up by the alternation of arches and pediments over the service cubicles is repeated above the styling stations. Here, the pediments and arches also contain fluorescent task lighting.

APPENDICES

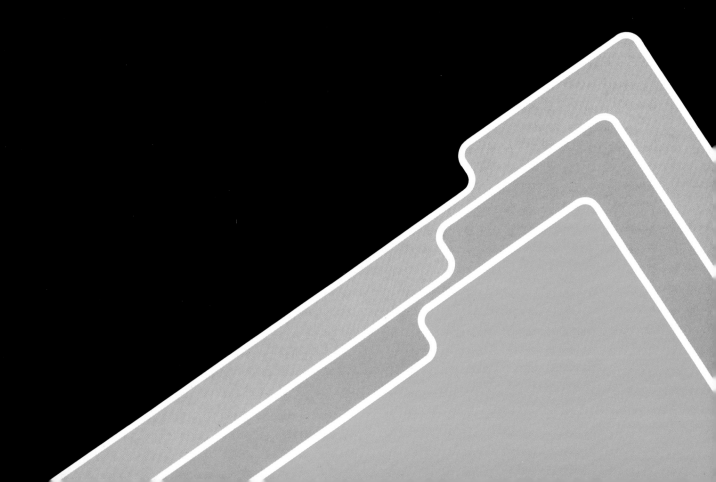

NEW FULL LINE DEPARTMENT STORES

FIRST AWARD   Bloomingdale's,
"The Falls",
Miami, Florida
Designed by Hambrecht Terrell
International

HONORABLE MENTION   Macy's,
Aventura Mall,
Miami, Florida
Designed by CNI International

HONORABLE MENTION   Burdines,
Oaks Mall,
Gainesville, Florida
Designed by Walker/Group, Inc.

RENOVATED FULL LINE DEPARTMENT STORES

HONORABLE MENTION   Carson, Pirie, Scott,
Randhurst Shopping Center,
Mount Prospect, Illinois
Designed by CNI International

HONORABLE MENTION   Macy's,
Del Monte Shopping Center,
Monterey, California
Designed by Store Planning Associates

Soft Goods Specialty Stores

FIRST AWARD
Burdines,
Coconut Grove, Florida
Designed by Walker/Group, Inc.

HONORABLE MENTION
L. L. Bean,
Freeport, Maine
Designed by Retail Planning Associates

HONORABLE MENTION
Parisian,
Madison Square Mall,
Huntsville, Alabama
Designed by Schafer Associates

Hard Goods Specialty Stores

HONORABLE MENTION
ServiStar,
Longview Texas
Designed by Retail Planning
Associates, Inc.

HONORABLE MENTION
Robert Floyd,
Palm Desert Town Center
Palm Desert, California
Designed by Naomi Leff and
Associates, Inc.

Department Store Floor Renovations

FIRST AWARD
Younkers,
Des Moines, Iowa
Designed by Schafer Associates

HONORABLE MENTION
Rich's,
Cumberland Mall,
Atlanta, Georgia
Designed by CNI International

HONORABLE MENTION
I. Magnin,
Union Square,
San Francisco, California
Designed by Walker/Group, Inc.

General Merchandise Stores

FIRST AWARD
Perry Ellis,
New York, New York
Designed by Hambrecht Terrell
International

HONORABLE MENTION
Collar Bar,
Boulevard Mall,
Las Vegas, Nevada
Designed by Planned Expansion
Group, Inc.

HONORABLE MENTION
Nathan Alan, Fine Jewlery,
South Coast Plaza,
Costa Mesa, California
Designed by The Bannister Group

Small Stores

FIRST AWARD
Hair Sensations,
Aventura Mall,
Miami, Florida
Designed by R.T.R. Designs, Inc.

THE ISP/NRMA STORE INTERIOR DESIGN COMPETITION RULES AND REQUIREMENTS

Purpose:

To promote recognition of the value of good design interiors. To recognize the contributions of particular organizations and individuals.

Entry Requirements:

1. Stores must have been completed (opened for business) during the year previous to the competition date.

2. At least one member of the design team must be a current member of the Institute of Store Planners or have an application pending for membership.

3. Entries must be completed fully to the following instructions.

4. Only one submission is permitted per category per entrant.

5. Entries must be received prior to the end of the business day on October 15 of the previous year.

Return of Entries:

1. All entries become the property of the Institute of Store Planners and the National Retail Merchants Association and will not be returned.

2. The Institute of Store Planners and the National Retail Merchants Association will be showing slides from this competition throughout the following year. Credits will be given to the store and the designers. If you wish your slides *not* to be used, please so indicate on the entry form.

Awards

1. One winner and two honorable mentions per category.

2. One store out of all the entries will be awarded "GRAND PRIZE".

3. Judges may change categories of individual entries if deemed appropriate.

4. Winning entries and honorable mentions will receive a certificate.

5. Winners in each category will receive an inscribed mounted plaque.

6. Awards will be presented by the ISP at the NRMA Store Planning, Design & Visual Merchandising Conference held in New York City. ISP members not participating in the conference can attend the presentation luncheon at the same price as the attendees. (Details of this event will be publicized separately.)

7. Award winners should be notified by November 1.

Jury

Judges of the competition include highly respected store designers, retailers, and acadamecians.

General Instructions

1. This is a concealed identification competition. Each entrant is responsible for ensuring that his name is placed on the registration form and nowhere else. Identification is controlled through the registration number which must be noted on all pages and all slides.

2. All entries must be in the 8½" x 11" format and inserted in a three ring binder as described herein.

3. Should an entry receive an award and be used for publication, all credits and other information will be taken from the registration form, project description, and other information contained in the entry. By submitting an entry, an entrant acknowledges that all information is accurate and that he has the right to publish this material.

4. These instructions may be used for entry to as many categories as desired by photocopying the registration form.

5. Entries should be packaged carefully and sent to:
   ISP/NRMA STORE INTERIOR DESIGN COMPETITION
   INSTITUTE OF STORE PLANNERS
   211 East 43rd Street, Suite 1601
   New York, NY 10017
   Entries must arrive before the end of the business day on October 15.

The Institute of Store Planners (ISP) is an organization dedicated to providing professional growth for its members while providing a service to the public through the improvement of the retail environment.

Membership of the Institute consists of professional store planners and designers, associate store planners, visual merchandisers, students, educators, as well as contractors and suppliers to the industry.

The Institute was founded in 1961 as a non-profit organization registered in the state of New York. It now has over 1,000 members who meet regularly in ten cities in the United States and Canada.

In addition to providing critics and lecturers for store planning and design courses at college level, the Institute also sponsors design contests and store planning seminars.

Meetings are held monthly at most of the Chapter and City Center locations where speakers are invited to present their work or product for the information of the members. Panel discussions, professional debate, and social activities enhance the fellowship of common interests.

A newsletter is published quarterly by the International Executive and various newsletters are also published by the Chapters.

For further information, contact the ISP Chapter or Center most convenient to you.

Chapters

INSTITUTE OF STORE PLANNERS
New York City Chapter
P.O. Box 538, Grand Central Station
New York, NY 10163

INSTITUTE OF STORE PLANNERS
Chicago Chapter
P.O. Box 3446, Merchandise Mart
Chicago, IL 60654

INSTITUTE OF STORE PLANNERS
San Francisco Chapter
P.O. Box 1216
San Francisco, CA 94101

INSTITUTE OF STORE PLANNERS
Charlotte Chapter
P.O. Box 221051
Charlotte, NC 28222

INSTITUTE OF STORE PLANNERS
Los Angeles Chapter
P.O. Box 5196
Sherman Oaks, CA 91423

INSTITUTE OF STORE PLANNERS
St. Louis Center
P.O. Box 16241
St. Louis, MO 63105

City Centers

INSTITUTE OF STORE PLANNERS
Ft. Lauderdale/Miami Center
P.O. Box 630041
Miami, FL 33163

INSTITUTE OF STORE PLANNERS
Boston Center
P.O. Box 506, Essex Station
Boston, MA 02112

INSTITUTE OF STORE PLANNERS
Honolulu Center
P.O. Box 61673
Honolulu, HI 96822

INSTITUTE OF STORE PLANNERS
Toronto Center
Designer's Walk
168 Bedford Road
Toronto, Ontario, CANADA M5R 2K9

INSTITUTE OF STORE PLANNERS
Columbus City Center
P.O. Box 16437
Columbus, OH 43216

INSTITUTE OF STORE PLANNERS
Atlanta City Center
P.O. Box 56964
Atlanta, GA 30343

The National Retail Merchants Association (NRMA), based in New York City, is the largest trade association in the United States dedicated to research and education in general merchandise retailing—the most comprehensive organization for retail management.

A not-for-profit organization, NRMA serves retail firms of all sizes in the United States and around the world. Members include chains, department stores, mass merchandisers, specialty stores, and independent retailers.

When established in 1911, NRMA stated its mission as follows and it remains true today:

- to concentrate opinions upon matters affecting the economy and well-being of the industry
- to foster research, education, development and study
- to gather, collect and disseminate information and statistical data
- to distribute articles, treatises, periodicals and books particularly related to the distribution of goods at retail

Since 1911, retailers worldwide have been attracted to the benefits of NRMA membership. Today, U.S. store members number around 45,000 and distribute $150 billion in goods and services to consumers. The International Division serves over 5,000 stores in 50 countries abroad. Also included in the membership are associate members who provide services, equipment and merchandise to retailers.

What NRMA Offers

1. **Expertise**
   Professional counsel and assistance are available on all aspects of retail management from a vast merchandising complex to a single store.

2. **Ideas**
   One-on-one consultation is available between NRMA's professional staff and store personnel. Meetings, seminars and conferences in every area from advertising to technology offer ideas on the latest trends.

3. **Education**
   Conferences, seminars, and workshops around the country discuss in detail all facets of retailing.

4. **Information**
   Members can receive valuable and authoritative publications concerning every aspect of specialty, independent, mass merchandising, and department store management and operation.

5. **Research**
   Major studies chart and appraise retailing's ever-changing course.

6. **Resources**
   A constantly expanding library of NRMA literature is at member's disposal.

7. **Inspiration**
   An annual convention and trade exposition is held every January in New York City attracting delegates from around the globe. Major topics of worldwide importance are addressed by industry leaders and top economists.

8. **Trends**
With membership—subscription to *STORES*—a stimulating, highly-acclaimed monthly magazine filled with authoritative articles on the latest retailing developments.

9. **Clout**
The Washington staff conducts a continuous program to help make our government responsive to the needs of both retailers and consumers and aids members in interpreting the results.

10. **Group benefits**
Membership advantages include: group life, medical and workmen's compensation insurance plans; check guarantee program; group bank card program; leasing and location advisory service; transportation management program and auto rental discounts.

Professional Staff

NRMA committees and boards are supported by a professional staff which is organized along the lines of a well-run general merchandise store with an executive responsible for each of the major divisions: Credit Management, Information Systems, Financial Executives, Merchandising, Operations, Personnel and Sales Promotion-Marketing.

These divisional executives keep abreast of the latest developments in their particular fields of expertise. They initiate research studies, publish books and periodicals, and arrange for conferences, seminars and symposiums as well as providing individual consultation services to members.

How NRMA Functions

Direction and guidance come from the membership, through elected officers, directors, and an extensive committee system. Committees and boards of directors are composed of representatives from a cross section of the membership.

The NRMA Board of Directors is elected by the membership and is composed of over 100 retail executives representing stores of all sizes and types throughout the United States and other countries as well.

NRMA recognizes the importance of the independent stores which comprise the fastest growing segment of NRMA membership and so has created an Independent Stores Board of Directors made up of individual entrepreneurs.

For more information on the National Retail Merchants Association write to:

National Retail Merchants Association

100 West 31st Street,
New York, New York 10001
Phone: (212) 244-8780
Telex: INT'l 220-883-TAUR

Washington D.C. Office:
1000 Connecticut Avenue NW, 20036
Telephone: (202) 223-8250

INDICES

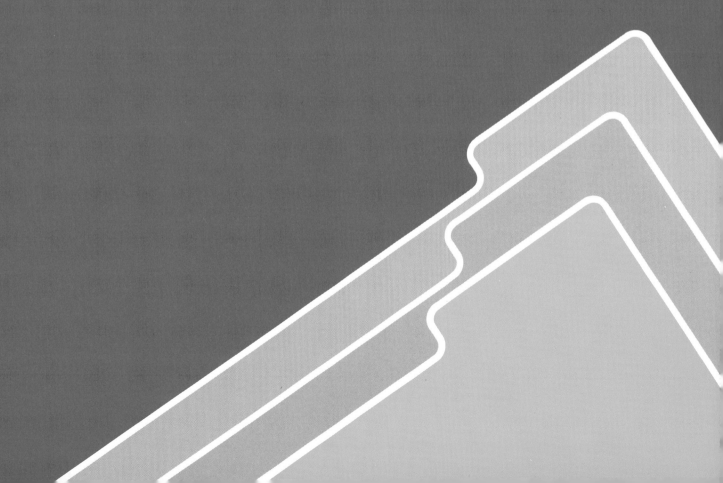

Design Firms

INDEX II

DESIGNERS

INDEX III

DECORATORS

INDEX IV

CONTRACTORS/ SUPPLIERS

project: G. B. Harb & Son, Los Angeles
design firm: L. A. Design
carpet: Royal Tartan by Bentley
photographer: Leland Lee

DuPont ANTRON® XL Nylon for low
maintenance and high performance

STEP INTO QUALITY

From the moment a customer walks in . . .
to the sale . . . there's a sense of quiet elegance
and high fashion with Bentley commercial carpets.

Step into quality when you choose Bentley
designer solids and patterns. Call your Bentley
Store Planning Specialist for a look
at high fashion, performance and style.

Quick delivery available for custom colors.

BENTLEY

BENTLEY MILLS, INC.
14641 E. Don Julian Road
City of Industry, CA 91746

818-333-4585
714-598-9768
800-423-4709

Display The Natural Way

Create original displays with Lundia's all natural MDL fixtures. The crisp Scandinavian design and the richness of solid wood give you the basis for a good-looking and practical fixture for all merchandise categories.

Whether it's toys or housewares, ceramics or wine, merchandise moves when you combine MDL shelving fixtures with your imagination. Over 60 standard combinations of height, depth and width will fit into your most creative arrangements. And those seasonal changes are simple with MDL. Easy set up and rearrangement is a Lundia trademark.

Make MDL a part of your merchandising plan. Ask for Lundia's free idea brochure today.

MDL
MERCHANDISE DISPLAY LINE

Send me your MDL idea brochure!

Name _____

Title _____

Company _____

Address _____

City _____

State _____

Zip _____ Phone _____

686

LUNDIA
The World's Record Holders ®
Lundia
600 Capitol Way
Jacksonville, IL 62650
217/243-8585

One week's signs in less than a day!

Your new Sign Shop!

Store Signing enters the Electronic Age

Clean, fast, and incredibly cost-effective, the PACC® System II computerized signing system renders all other sign making methods obsolete.

Combining an IBM PC with a "high resolution" printer and Reynolds' exclusive field tested software, PACC eliminates messy inks, cleaners, and chemicals associated with traditional and phototypesetting methods.

PACC will dramatically reduce your labor costs. And PACC can transmit all your signs to branch stores via telephone or microwave, saving distribution costs.

The new PACC sign shop will enable you to gain a competitive edge by making your benefit copy signing:
- more effective and profitable
- more controllable and timely
- support your ad copy
- easier than ever before!

PACC®
Printasign's Advanced Communication Concept

 REYNOLDS PRINTASIGN CO. / 9830 San Fernando Road, Pacoima, California 91331 / (818) 899-5281

TORQUEFUSION™

THE SHOWOFF!

TORQUEFUSION™

We hate to showoff. But in order for you to appreciate the amazing benefits of our new TorqueFusion™ Acrylic Displays, we had to. Just a little.

We make your product look great. Our crystal clear acrylic enhances your products from every angle. And our hand crafted polished edges provide added customer protection. TorqueFusion™ eliminates tops, bottoms, backs, and load bearing glue seams used in standard display unit construction methods today.

We'll be around a long time. We guarantee it. Using threaded fasteners, TorqueFusion™ Displays provide

Fashioned In Acrylic Fastened With Steel

both strength and durability unparalleled in the market today. However, if a replacement shelf is ever needed, simply unscrew the threaded fasteners and replace it. Sound simple. It is.

We're ready to go on arrival. Torque-Fusion™ Displays are shipped completely assembled. Simply uncrate it and place your merchandise.

We have it now at DesignLab. Torque-Fusion™ Displays. The Display Fixture line for the future, today. For further information contact Don Ballard at 800/222-6408.

DesignLab

DesignLab / 3023 Asbury Avenue / Charlotte, N.C. 28206 / Phone 704-376-2769

Visual Merchandising & Store Design

Look to the Leader

Look to VISUAL MERCHANDISING & STORE DESIGN magazine for comprehensive coverage of store design and merchandise presentation as applied by retailers across the country. From apparel and non-apparel specialty stores to department stores, mass merchandisers and discount operations, you'll have at your fingertips the source of the most innovative techniques as applied by such retailing diversity.

Look to the leader that will take you through 1985 equipped to handle the challenges ahead. Twelve informative issues will expand your knowledge of fixtures, lighting, mannequins, signage, ceiling systems, architectural decor and design materials and more. Look to the leader that will keep you a leader in the years to come.

YES, enter my subscription to **Visual Merchandising & Store Design** for term indicated:

	US	Outside US
☐ 1 yr/12 issues	**$21.00**	**$32.00**
☐ 2 yr/24 issues	**$35.00**	**$57.00**
☐ 3 yr/36 issues	**$46.00**	**$79.00**

☐ Payment enclosed
☐ Bill Me
☐ Charge to credit card

☐ Mastercard   ☐ VISA   ☐ AMEX

Card No. _____ Expiration _____

Signature _____

Payment must be in US funds. Check to be drawn on a US bank.

Above rates based on surface mail. Air Mail postage would be additional.

Send with name and address to:

Visual Merchandising & Store Design

407 Gilbert Ave., Cincinnati, OH 45202-U.S.A